Anonymous

The Cape Fear and Yadkin Valley Railway:

Its origin, construction, connections, and extensions: Embracing descriptive and statistical notices of cities, towns, villages, and stat

Anonymous

The Cape Fear and Yadkin Valley Railway:
Its origin, construction, connections, and extensions: Embracing descriptive and statistical notices of cities, towns, villages, and stat

ISBN/EAN: 9783337731311

Printed in Europe, USA, Canada, Australia, Japan

Cover: Foto ©ninafisch / pixelio.de

More available books at **www.hansebooks.com**

THE
CAPE FEAR AND YADKIN VALLEY
RAILWAY.

(FROM MT. AIRY, AT THE BASE OF THE BLUE RIDGE,
TO WILMINGTON, N. C.)

Its Origin, Construction, Connections, and Extensions.

EMBRACING

DESCRIPTIVE AND STATISTICAL NOTICES OF CITIES, TOWNS, VILLAGES,
AND STATIONS; INDUSTRIES, AGRICULTURAL, MANUFACTURING,
AND MINERAL RESOURCES; SCENERY OF THE ROUTE;
TRANSMONTANE EXTENSION, &c.

Illustrated with Engravings made from Photographs.

ORGANIZATION

OF THE

Cape Fear and Yadkin Valley Railway Company.

1889.

JULIUS A. GRAY	PRESIDENT.
J. W. FRY	GEN'L SUP'T.
ROGER P. ATKINSON	CHIEF ENGINEER.
JNO. M. ROSE	SECRETARY.
R. W. BIDGOOD	AUDITOR.
JAS. R. WILLIAMS	TREASURER.
W. E. KYLE	G. F. AND P. A.
GEO. M. ROSE	ATTORNEY.

DIRECTORS:

K. M. MURCHISON, New York.
JNO. M. WORTH, Asheboro, N. C.
W. A. LASH, Walnut Cove, N. C.
JULIUS A. GRAY, Greensboro, N. C.
G. W. WILLIAMS, Wilmington, N. C.
JNO. D. WILLIAMS, Fayetteville, N. C.
CHAS. P. STOKES, Richmond, Va.
W. A. MOORE, Mt. Airy, N. C.
J. TURNER MOREHEAD, Leaksville, N. C.
D. W. C. BENBOW, Greensboro, N. C.
ROBT. T. GRAY, Raleigh, N. C.
E. J. LILLY, Fayetteville, N. C.

GENERAL OFFICES,
FAYETTEVILLE, N. C.

PRESIDENT'S OFFICE,
GREENSBORO, N. C.

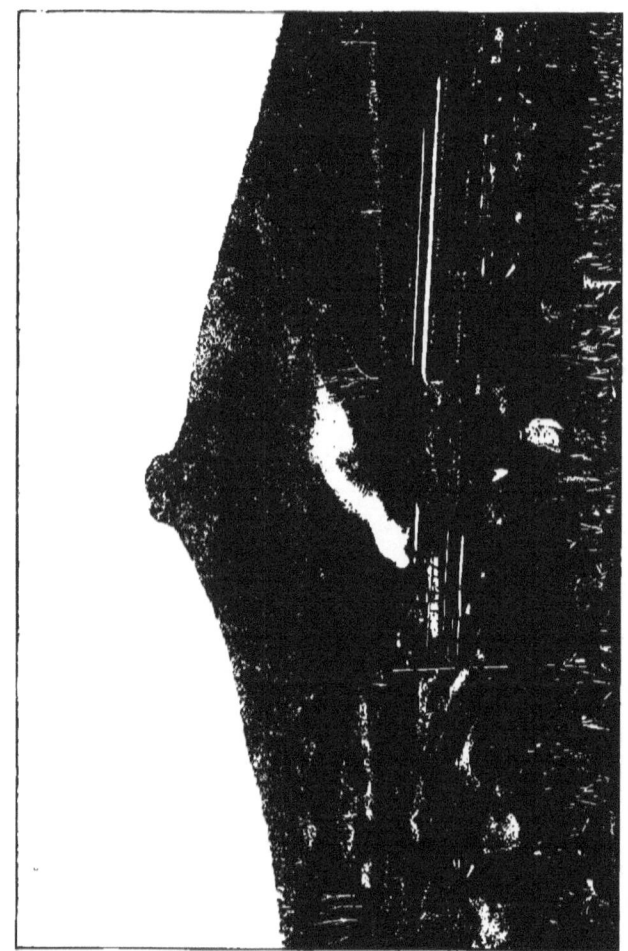

PILOT MOUNTAIN, FROM NEAR PINNACLE STATION.

Cape Fear and Yadkin Valley Railway System.

Its Inception ⊛ Gradual Progress ⊛ Final Completion.

THE uninterrupted progress of the Cape Fear and Yadkin Valley Railway, and its unrivaled prosperity and steadily increasing traffic since the granting of its present charter by the General Assembly of 1879, were only to be expected in the full development and completion of a railway system which occupied the minds of progressive and thoughtful men even as far back as the earlier days of the present century.

This system embodied the great ulterior object of opening to the markets of the world the rich territory of the Upper Yadkin Valley by connection with Fayetteville as the head of navigation on the Cape Fear River. Even at as distant a period as 1815 the immense advantages to accrue from the fruition of this project caught and fixed the attention of leading men in the legislature, and such connection by canal was favorably reported and even undertaken; but the obstacles opposing themselves proved insurmountable to the crude progress of that day, and the work was abandoned. But inherent in the Cape Fear and Yadkin Valley system was the very life of North Carolina's internal improvement—again and again to revive and make itself felt until the time was ripe for the full accomplishment of the great and comprehensive design. Nearly sixty years ago a charter was obtained, and ground broken at Fayetteville for the building of the Cape Fear, Yadkin and Pee Dee Railroad; but it was met by difficulties—insuperable at that period—of a want of familiarity with railroad work, the disinclination of a sparse population to hazard their means in what they regarded as a doubtful experiment, and the inability of the State to furnish resources for the extension of the work. For twenty years the Cape Fear and Yadkin Valley system lay dormant, within which period was pushed forward to completion the then whole railroad mileage of North Carolina: the Raleigh and Gaston, the Wilmington and Weldon, now forming a great link of one hundred and sixty-two miles in the Atlantic Coast Line, and the North Carolina Railroad, at present leased by the Richmond and Danville Railroad Company, and making an important part of that extensive system.

In 1852 a charter was granted for the Western (Coal Fields) Railroad, extending from Fayetteville west through the counties of Cumberland, Moore, Harnett and Chatham, which, with the large amount of stock taken therein by the State, and by the aid of liberal subscriptions from the county of Cumberland, the town of Fayetteville and individual stockholders, was built to Egypt, progressing no farther than that point when the outbreak of the war suspended all further operations. Imperfectly worked as they were, the coal mines of Egypt, and the Western Railroad, with its facilities for transportation, proved of incalculable service to the Confederate Government in the struggle of four years which ensued.

Fourteen years elapsed. The political rehabilitation and reconstruction of the seceded States had been accomplished; and again this great system of State internal improvement and material development demanded recognition and received it at the hands of the General Assembly of 1879, which, by an act ratified February 25th, authorized the consolidation of the Western Railroad with the Mt. Airy Railroad, and changed the name of the corporation to that of Cape Fear and Yadkin Valley Railway Company. At the next session of the General Assembly, and again in that of 1883, the State surrendered her interests in the road, with some needed concessions, to a company of private citizens, who have been building wisely and vigorously ever since the affairs of the corporation passed into their hands.

Almost immediately after assuming the management of the Cape Fear and Yadkin Valley Railway, April 6th, 1881, the present company entered into a contract with the directors of the Fayetteville and Florence Railroad for the extension over its graded road-bed of the Cape Fear and Yadkin Valley to Shoe Heel, intersecting the Carolina Central Railway at that point, and continuing on to the State line. Simultaneously the work of construction was pushed westward, trains were running into the city of Greensboro on the day of the annual meeting of stockholders in 1884, and early in autumn of the same year the southern extension tapped the Carolina Central Railroad at Shoe Heel (now Maxton), in Robeson County.

On the 26th of July, 1883, a contract had been made with the directors of the Southern Pacific Railway for the grading, tracklaying and equipment of that road from the State line to Bennettsville, S. C.; and by the 5th of December, 1884, the great work was completed—a distance of one hundred and fifty-four miles from Bennettsville to Greensboro, with ample rolling

PILOT MOUNTAIN, FROM DALTON, N. C.

stock, station-houses, warehouses, and freight accommodations—while at the latter city convenient connection was made with the Richmond and Danville Railroad. But the green hills of Piedmont were now just in sight, while the stalwart mountaineers of the Blue Ridge were waiting with eager eye and heart intent for the advent of this agent of civilization and development. With every mile of grading and construction the difficulties of engineering were multiplied; but there was little pause in the work of extension, and very soon the road wound its way through the suburbs of Greensboro westward, passing under the North Carolina Railroad within the limits of the city. On the 20th of June, 1888, excursion trains carried thousands of people from every point along the line of the Cape Fear and Yadkin Valley Railway to participate in the ceremonies incident to the celebration of Mt. Airy's railroad connection with the great outer world—the beautiful village lying under the shadow of the towering chain of the Blue Ridge.

A branch road had in the meantime been laid to Millboro—in the vicinity of the extensive factories at Franklinville and other points on Deep River—connecting with the main line at Factory Junction, twelve miles east of Greensboro; and on the 28th of December, 1888, the Madison Branch, extending from Stokesdale to Madison, traversing a fertile portion of Rockingham county, had been so nearly completed as to admit of running a regular train schedule to within a few hundred yards of the town.

It is proper to say here that all the work of construction within the past five years has been performed by contract by the North State Improvement Company, incorporated in the year 1883, and composed of men of high character and prominence in business circles, of which John D. Williams, of Fayetteville, is president; and the traveling public cheerfully bear witness to the fidelity with which the work has been done.

A very significant fact in the history of the Cape Fear and Yadkin Valley Railway it may not be amiss to note before proceeding to a compilation of the descriptive gazette of the mineral, manufacturing and agricultural resources of the different sections of North Carolina which it reaches and renders accessible to the world's markets: no other railway enterprise has interfered with its progress, or lessened the need of its completion. During the past ten years of its present name, directory and management, together with a few years previous thereto, the Western Division of the North Carolina Railroad has been completed, that portion of the Carolina Central which had long remained as a gap between Wadesboro and Charlotte has been laid, the Salem Branch of the Piedmont Air-Line has been built, the Raleigh and Augusta Air-Line has made connection with the Carolina Central at

Hamlet, the Wilson Short Cut, a branch of the Atlantic Coast Line, has been finished—and other less important branches, extending into Virginia and South Carolina, have been constructed or are in process of construction. Not one has discredited the wisdom, weakened the importance, or proved a serious obstacle to the completion of the Cape Fear and Yadkin Valley Railway, which—crossing the chief water-ways of the State and forming a direct line through some of the finest region of the three geological divisions of North Carolina—bisects it from northwest to southeast, aiming to make final connection by the shortest route with the great railway highway at Cincinnati, and combining finally that most admirable feature of railroading which reaches out and penetrates the undeveloped back country, with its own great seaport for an outlet, with all its advantages to hundreds of miles of interior of its shipping, diversified manufactures and commerce. Lastly, it is noteworthy that the increase of business of the Cape Fear and Yadkin Valley Railway has kept pace with every mile of road built. No station along the line has failed to swell the receipts; no branch has proven unremunerative for the outlay; and the reports at every stockholders' meeting demonstrate a largely augmenting volume of business.

FRONT STREET, WILMINGTON, N. C.

Eastern Division.

FROM WILMINGTON TO FAYETTEVILLE—EIGHTY-ONE AND SEVEN-TENTHS MILES.

WILMINGTON.

WILMINGTON, the eastern terminus of the Cape Fear and Yadkin Valley Railway, the largest town in North Carolina, and one of the most important ports on the South Atlantic coast, is situated on the east side of the Cape Fear River, and (air-line) twenty-six miles from its bar. In a direct line the city is distant but little over six miles from the ocean.

More than a century ago a devastating storm formed what is now known as New Inlet; this breach did not show itself in the channel until 1850, when the Government made an appropriation of $100,000. Careful engineering showed two water shoals and exits in the channel, and the draught of water was reduced from twenty-two to twelve feet.

To remedy this evil the Government has expended from 1870 up to June 30th, 1888, something over $1,851,000, with substantial success, securing from fourteen to fourteen and five-tenths least depth of water at the main bar entrance, with a channel of sixteen feet depth twenty-eight miles farther to Wilmington. Combining this depth with average rise of tide of four and five-tenths feet at the bar, and two and five-tenths feet at the city, loaded vessels with a draught of sixteen feet can go from Wilmington to the ocean on a single tide any day of the year.

From the time this work of the Government was commenced until 1887, the total commerce of Wilmington had increased from $13,500,000 per annum to nearly $20,000,000, and its foreign exports alone from less than $1,500,000 to over $8,000,000. The carrying out of the recommendations of Captain Bixby, Chief Engineer, that the dike be finished south to Zeke Island, so as to secure Smith's Island from further erosion by the ocean, with the widening of the river channels to their full dimensions of two hundred and seventy feet, will probably restore the original full depth of water. The company's shipping facilities at Point Peter will be good, as sixteen feet depth of water can be gotten there on tide. Their terminal facilities will be first-class, with train yards of ample accommodations to transport their freight to Point Peter, where lighters will carry it to the city wharves of the company.

COALING STATION.

In the descriptive gazette of the Upper Cape Fear and Deep River Division, a full report has been made of the work now going on at the Egypt coal mines, giving an output of three hundred tons per diem. The careful sketch of the transmontane extension, which concludes this hand-book, makes it certain that the connection of the Cape Fear and Yadkin Valley Railway with the Norfolk and Western will give it large freights from the coal fields of Southwest Virginia and Southeast Kentucky. This will make necessary a branch road to Southport, which offers exceptional advantages as the great coaling station on the South Atlantic coast. Vessels putting into Newport News for coal go in one hundred and eighty miles, and out the same distance; Southport, from the beaten track, is twenty-three miles in and out. Such unsurpassed advantages require no comment.

MANUFACTURING.

The manufacturing establishments are numerous, and many of them extensive, classified as follows:—

- 5 steam saw and planing mills.
- 3 sash, blind and door factories.
- 1 ice factory.
- 3 machine shops and foundries.
- 2 fertilizer manufactories.
- 1 factory of pine wool matting fibre and pine wool cotton bagging.
- 3 establishments for the manufacture of clothing.
- 1 ladies' and children's underwear factory.
- 3 carriage factories.
- 3 soda water and beer bottling establishments.
- 1 chemical company.
- 1 paint and oil manufactory.
- 1 dyeing establishment.
- 1 cotton mill.
- 1 stocking factory.
- 1 marble works.
- 1 creosote and acid works.
- 1 naval store manufactory.
- 2 packers and refiners of tar.
- 2 rice mills.
- 4 grain mills.
- 3 candy factories.
- 1 alcohol manufactory.

This makes a total of 45 manifold and valuable industries.

CITY HALL, WILMINGTON, N. C.

NEW INDUSTRIES.

The Acme Manufacturing Company, occupying extensive buildings a few miles from the city, has developed a new industry which is destined, probably, to prove a very important one. From the green straw of the pine (a material which exists in inexhaustible quantities through all that section of the State), they manufacture a fibre which distinguished surgical authority has pronounced of exceptional value in the dressing of wounds; carpet matting and bedding are also made therefrom, which are durable, handsome, and free from insects, to which the balsamic odor of the pine leaf is peculiarly obnoxious. But the most important branch of this industry, in a commercial point of view, is the manufacture of pine fibre cotton bagging, which, it is claimed, is in all respects equal to jute bagging. From this pine leaf is also extracted an oil, antiseptic and possessed of medicinal virtues. The Carolina Oil and Creosoting Company extensively manufactures creosote oil from ordinary pine wood, and effectively prepares piling and timber against rot and the ravages of other destructive agencies. The timber, after being subjected to a process which thoroughly carbonizes it, is placed in creosoting cylinders, where it is thoroughly impregnated with the oil, and is sent out for effective use for an almost unlimited time. The company has a capacity of about thirty thousand linear feet per day. There are, besides, the Wilmington and Champion Cotton Compress Companies, occupying magnificent structures in the business part of the city, with about an equal capacity of from twelve hundred to fifteen hundred bales per day of twenty-four hours. This preparation for shipment and movement of cotton, it will be readily seen, makes in the aggregate an immense volume of business in the employment of hands, the transactions at the banking houses, and the placing of a large amount of ready money in circulation. The completion of the Cape Fear and Yadkin Valley Railway will increase the area of cotton production, and will thus benefit Wilmington as a market for that staple.

THE GROWTH OF WILMINGTON.

The city of Wilmington is steadily increasing in population (and consequently in dwellings and other structures), wealth, manufacturing and commerce. No better demonstration could be made of the enlargement of the city's limits and of the number of those whose business or pleasure carries them from one portion to the other day by day, than the fact that, while one street-railway was discontinued for the want of adequate support, that now in operation is paying what would be a satisfactory dividend on more than double its stock. The best informed of its citizens estimate that the census of 1890 will give it a population of about twenty-seven thousand, the increase being mostly white.

Exports.

The following official table gives the amount of exports in its leading articles for the year 1888:—

Cotton (bales)	162,993
Spirits turpentine (casks)	63,473
Rosin (barrels)	246,566
Tar (barrels)	63,163
Crude turpentine (barrels)	21,572
Timber and lumber (feet)	36,679,509
Pitch (barrels)	8,489
Peanuts (bushels)	40,397
Cotton goods (packages)	1,514
Shingles	6,663,980

Besides the leading articles above enumerated, there is a large export trade, foreign and coastwise, of cotton seed and cotton-seed oil, rice, peanuts, peas, garden truck, melons and other fruits, &c.

Shipping.

The improvements made and being made by the Government work in the harbor have been followed by a marked increase in the size of the vessels entering port. An average tonnage for foreign sail has been raised from two hundred to four hundred tons, though many vessels register as high as one thousand or twelve hundred tons, with foreign steamers ranging from eight hundred to seventeen hundred tons. The arrivals in port for the year 1888 were as follows:—

Foreign steamers		24	26,083 tons.
" sail		107	42,742 "
Total		131	68,825 "
American steamers		95	76,567 tons.
" sail		144	40,251 "
		239	116,818 "

The New York and Wilmington Steamship Company's notably improved business is a gratifying evidence of the city's increasing prosperity. The line is now doing all that it can manage, and will undoubtedly in the near future be forced to enlarge its service and transportation.

TURPENTINE FOREST.

Fisheries.

But the future, after all, is to develop the great industry of Wilmington—the cultivation of its oyster-fields and fishing-grounds. With as fine an oyster as is to be found in the world within a few miles of their doors, the housekeepers at the market, unless very particular, are forced to put up with a small, inferior oyster, as the genuine New River oyster is obtained in only limited quantities, being transported across country in carts, and is eagerly bought up by *restaurateurs*, to be generally served on the half-shell, where they are perfection, unless surpassed by the "Blue Points" of the New York market. From Federal Point, along the coast for eighty or ninety miles, with a width of from one to two miles, is a continuous sound filled with vast oyster-beds thousands of acres in extent, and abounding in innumerable choice fish of every description. Once connect this immense field for a remunerative industry with Wilmington by rail (the distance is only a few miles), and the city would straightway fall heir to a profitable business amounting to hundreds of thousands of dollars, and eventually millions, annually. Oysters, both fresh and canned, would be transported over its lines of railway, seining stations would at once be established all along the sound, and deep-sea fishing would be greatly increased. The business would find eager customers at all the interior towns on the Cape Fear and Yadkin Valley Railway, whose people have hitherto been shut out from a good fish and oyster market, and who covet these luxuries even more than the dwellers along the coast.

The Water-Supply.

Wilmington is supplied with water by the Clarendon Water-Works Company, whose plant is situated immediately in front of the historic old mansion of Cornelius Harnett. It is the combined standpipe and direct-pressure system, with three duplex Worthington pumps of a total capacity of three million gallons in twenty-four hours, running through about twelve miles of main pipe from four to twelve inches in diameter, to which is attached one hundred and five public and seventeen private fire-hydrants. The average daily consumption of water is about five hundred thousand gallons. The company has also commenced the boring of an artesian well, which, at the close of winter, had attained a depth of five hundred and fifty feet.

Wharf and Terminal Facilities.

The company has recently purchased property for terminus of road at Point Peter, just at the confluence of Cape Fear and North East Rivers, with a wharf front of thirteen hundred and sixty feet. Contracts have been let, the work of pile-driving for the company's wharves was commenced on the 15th of March, and the work will be completed by 1st of May.

Valuable property has also been bought in Wilmington, adjoining the Ocean Steamship Wharf, of one hundred feet under shelter, with one hundred and thirty-seven feet front adjacent, the whole running back to Water Street, and including two valuable brick buildings. The transfer of passengers and freight from the terminus of the road to the company's wharves in Wilmington will be made by steam-ferry and lighters.

It is confidently expected that the eastern extension will be completed by the close of the present year, which every branch of business in Wilmington will feel immediately most beneficially. Besides the increased facilities for obtaining timber offered to the workers in wood, and the new field opened for all descriptions of manufacturing, the merchants of Wilmington will enjoy great advantages in lower rates of freight, and will be enabled to sell almost any class of goods to country dealers at any point on the road as far west as Greensboro, as cheaply as they can be bought at Richmond or Baltimore.

WILMINGTON TO THE HEALTH OR PLEASURE SEEKER.

With a mean annual temperature of sixty-three degrees, and a mean humidity of fifty-seven degrees, Wilmington offers to the tourist, in a hygienic point of view, attractions not to be surpassed by any part of South Florida or Georgia. Here the winds hardly ever blow from one quarter for more than forty to forty-eight hours, it is nearly entirely free from fogs, and is as exempt from epidemic diseases as it is possible for a place to be. In a contracted area, embracing Southport and Wilmington, the climate is semi-tropical, and snow rarely ever falls. On the afternoon of February 21st, of this year, the slow-moving leaden clouds gave the people of Wilmington a treat, and great flakes fell thick and fast for an hour, covering the ground to the depth of an inch or two. The writer watched with much amusement the wild delight of young and old in their welcome of the rare visitor, and he was assured by one aged citizen, whose cheeks were aglow with the exercise, and his hat crushed in by a snowball, that they "hadn't had such a good snow in fifteen years." As a summer resort Wilmington offers to the tourist and the invalid advantages which are unparalleled by that of any other point on the Atlantic coast. Rapid and agreeable transit by shell road, steamer and railway has been provided to Carolina Beach, Wrightsville Sound and "The Rocks," at all three of which the hotel accommodations are excellent, and during the season that is daily witnessed which is possible nowhere else from Maine to Florida—the visitor is transported up to the very surf, to mingle with the

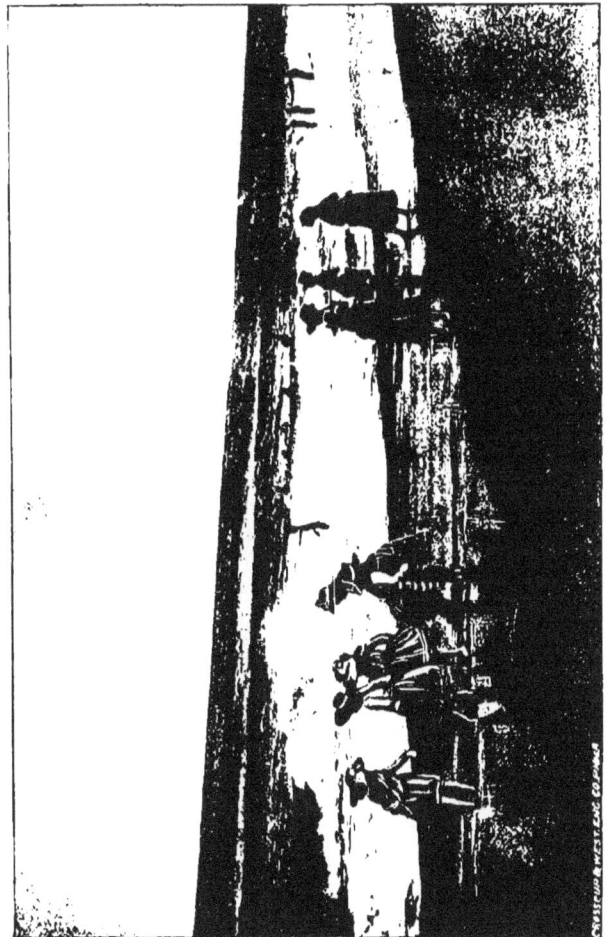

SURF BATHING, NEAR WILMINGTON, N. C.

sportive bathers, by the locomotive, which would almost seem to be striving to lave its heated sides in the tossing, foaming waves. The surf bathing is safe and delightful; the waters of the sound offer a wide area for yachting and sail-boating, while the fishing is superb—Spanish mackerel of great size, the blackfish, bluefish, pigfish, flounder and other species being caught in great numbers. The last General Assembly of North Carolina also fixed the permanent encampment of the State Guard at Wrightsville, assembling in July, which will prove an accession to the pleasant features of that resort during the season.

The hotel accommodations of the city of Wilmington will now compare favorably with those of any other city in the South. The Orton, an ornate and commodious edifice, recently constructed on North Front Street, with its elegantly furnished chambers, its parlors fitted up with every luxury, its exquisitely appointed dining-room, the careful and polite attention of its employés, and, most important of all, its perfect *cuisine*, offers to the voyager a pleasant house of rest during his journeyings, or to the invalid a beautiful home, supplied with every comfort during the months of winter, and crowned with every attraction during the heat of summer. The guests of the Orton Hotel have the privileges of the fishing and hunting of the Orton plantation, one of the princely possessions of the builder and owner of the hotel, Colonel K. M. Murchison, of New York. Here are about nine thousand acres of "preserved" land, upon which is situated the old homestead, and about it lingers still the aroma of an historic past, for here was once the capital of the Colony and the residence of the Royal Governors. Here, too, are the ruins of old St. Philip's Church, built in 1751, to which was presented a silver communion service by George III. of England; but the brier and the vine have possessed themselves of sculptured lintel and plinth, dank weeds invade the broken chancel, silence enwraps the crumbling wall, and the gray, majestic ruin is given up to "age and memories of eld."

THE CITY'S GOVERNMENT, &c.

The streets of the city are moderately well-lighted by both gas and electricity, while three steam fire-engines, with hook and ladder companies and numerous hose-reel teams, are relied upon to prevent a recurrence of the disastrous conflagrations which have twice within the past five years swept over the fairest portions of the city. Like all old towns, Wilmington lacks regularity and symmetry in its architecture. It can boast of but few public or private buildings notable for beauty or costliness, though there are many handsome churches and elegant private residences. But its City Hall and Opera House may well evoke the pride of any community, and challenge the admiration of the most finished connoisseur of correct and tasteful architecture. No finer specimen of the pure Doric exists in this country within the knowledge of the writer. Perfect in proportion, simple and graceful in unity of design, its exterior is accompanied by a fitting interior of lofty halls, broad passages and spacious chambers. The Opera House is a beautiful hall, capable of accommodating over one thousand persons.

MISCELLANEOUS.

The people of Wilmington are impulsive and warm-hearted, and hospitality to the stranger within their gates is to them an obligation as sacred as to the Arab in his tent; they never seem so happy as when welcoming and entertaining a convention or other large assemblage of visitors. Some of the most prominent business men of the South are influential leaders in the commercial circles of this community; and their legal bar, always distinguished for ability, now numbers some of the foremost men of the State.

The public and private schools are numerous and excellent, the municipal government is well administered, and the financial condition of the city excellent.

Excavations have been made for the new Government building on Front Street, which will be an imposing edifice—a great accession to the city's architecture.

At Wilmington are located the machine and construction shops of the Atlantic Coast Line Railroad (the most extensive in the South), turning out an immense amount of first-class work.

Besides the Cape Fear and Yadkin Valley Railway, Wilmington is the terminus of the Carolina Central Railway, the Wilmington, Columbia and Augusta Railroad, the Wilmington and Weldon Branch of the Atlantic Coast Line, and the Wilmington and Onslow Railroad (projected).

AGRICULTURAL AND TIMBER RESOURCES, &c.

Contiguous to Wilmington the land is very fertile: a clayey soil, impregnated with phosphatic matter, ocean salts, and alkalies, it was undoubtedly uplifted by the ocean in ages past. With even a slight admixture of organic matter, deeply plowed in, vegetation is rendered luxuriant, and nowhere are soil, climate, and atmospheric conditions more favorable to the trucker and market-gardener. Grapes are grown of delightful flavor, wonderful size and in boundless profusion, many of the varieties producing a second crop during the season. The Lower and Upper Cape Fear sections of the road embrace portions of the counties of New Hanover, Brunswick, Pender, Sampson, Bladen and Cumberland, and gradually rise from the sea level, by an easily ascending champaign, to an altitude of a little more than one hundred feet

A N. SOPPING RIVER SCENE, NEAR WINDSOR.

at Fayetteville. Lying directly upon the route of the line, portions of the country are sparsely settled, the land is thin, and generous crops are denied to the farmer. Along the water-courses, however—Black River, Cape Fear and the creeks, which are extensive and numerous—there is a rich alluvial soil, producing a magnificent yield in corn and cotton. All this area is subject to overflow in seasons of continuous rain; but, when spared this drawback to their returns, splendid harvests are reaped; and nowhere is to be found a better system of agriculture than exists in portions of the counties grouped under this heading.

The *flora* of this region is varied and exuberant; fifty-four different kinds of wood were found by actual observation in a piece of land comprising four acres—swamp, upland, and woods. In addition to dogwood (used in shuttle manufacturing), juniper, cypress (the material for the immense number of shingles shipped from Wilmington every year), poplar, and the white and water oaks, recent official figures have placed the amount of yellow-heart, long-leaf pine standing in this section, exclusive of Cumberland, at over one billion feet.

The completion of this division of the Cape Fear and Yadkin Valley Railway will therefore not only give an impetus to agriculture and the other elements of material prosperity, but it will render accessible a vast area of virgin timber land; and the sawyers of wood and the makers of lumber— the pioneers of new communities and increased population with every mile of railway extension everywhere—will plant their machinery on creek, valley and hillside, to secure the rich returns of these uncut forests, giving employment to hundreds, planting settlements, building villages, and infusing new life and enterprise into all that section.

The farmers of these lower counties, notably Pender, Sampson and Bladen, have always devoted much attention to the raising of fine stock, and the yearly exhibits of good horses, cattle, hogs and sheep, at the Sampson County Agricultural Fairs, attracted large crowds, and received favorable attention from all parts of the State.

The staple crops of this section are diversified and valuable: rice, peanuts, the early truck of the market-gardener (peas, beans, lettuce, radishes, cucumbers, salads, asparagus, &c.), sorghum cane (the area in which has greatly increased of late years), corn, cotton, oats and rye.

The grading and construction work on the road-bed of the Eastern Division is rapidly approaching completion—bridge-work, trestling, putting in of culverts, and all the other labor incident to placing the bed in readiness for track-laying; the stations, sidings and water-tanks have been nearly all located, and it is reasonably certain that at the date of this publication track-laying will have commenced.

THE BRIDGE OVER THE CAPE FEAR.

At Fayetteville, a few hundred yards below the county bridge, a new iron railroad bridge is now constructing by the company—four iron spans, the approaches one hundred and ninety feet each; the middle spans one hundred and fifty feet each; total length of bridge, six hundred and eighty feet.

A single-span iron bridge also crosses Black or South River on this route.

FAYETTEVILLE.

Here abides a people with a history. Here and there some quaint, oldtime building—a veritable landmark of the past—tells of its "vanished glories;" in the beautiful cemetery, whose dead sleep to the soft plashing of the waters of Cross Creek, the time-stained marble glints in the sunlight, and is flecked with the shifting shadows of the swaying elms, as it perpetuates the names and memories of the men oblivious now of all the triumphs of human achievement, but whose commanding abilities, spotless integrity and untiring energy made the Fayetteville of the olden time great in business and commerce.

Within a stone's throw of the accompanying illustration of Eccles Park, one finds the site of the abode of Flora McDonald, about whose name years but add to the pleasing romance which softens the rugged lines of history—the gifted heroine inseparably linked in the records of the past with every mention of the chivalrous but ill-starred Prince Charles Edward, whose devotion to the House of Stuart brought her from the shores of her native country, nearly a century and a half ago, to settle with a little band of friends and adherents, in this quiet, far-away spot in a new and untried land. Not a stone is left of the domicile which sheltered this noble Scotchwoman; but the spirit which inspired her and the little colony of followers has not abandoned the valleys and the hills which they made historic for all time; it lives still in the sturdiness of character, honesty, thrift and industry of their descendants, now multiplied into an intelligent population throughout the counties of Cumberland, Harnett, Moore, Richmond and Robeson.

A GREAT INLAND TRADE.

Fifty years ago Fayetteville controlled nearly all the inland trade of North Carolina, with a large part of that of portions of Tennessee and Virginia. The merchants of Wilmington were accumulating fortunes in plying a vast and lucrative business with the West Indies; and the Cape Fear River transportation of molasses, sugar, salt, iron, coffee and the goods of the Northern markets, to Fayetteville, the head of its navigation, was immense. Canvas-

OLD MARKET-HOUSE, FAYETTEVILLE, N. C.

topped wagons—drawn by two, four and six horses, with jingling bells, traversing hundreds of miles from across the Blue Ridge, winding over the red hills of the rugged country about the Pilot and the Suaratown Mountains—creaked slowly and heavily on, to the shout of driver and the crack of whip, towards Fayetteville—the Mecca of trade, the El Dorado of marvelous riches in merchandise. These wagons were nearly all laden with the products of their sections—butter, lard, bacon, beeswax, flour, hides, flaxseed, back-country whisky and brandy—carrying back in exchange goods for the country merchant and for home consumption; and they drove into the town in long lines, grouping themselves about the different places of business whence came the hum of traffic all day and often far into the night. The country tributary to Fayetteville was networked with plank roads to facilitate this great and continuous wagon travel, one line (the Western Plank Road) being one hundred and twenty miles in length. But the "iron horse" was more powerful than the road wagon, and a very large part of the back-country trade of Fayetteville was diverted into other channels, from causes which we need not go far to seek.

Note here that the Cape Fear and Yadkin Valley Railway system—conceived in the days of the wealth and prosperity of the tidewater and Upper Cape Fear section—lays the steel rail upon the disused old rut of this remunerative traffic, and its long trains bound with the swift life of steam-power over the route of the slow-toiling wagon caravan; from the seacoast to the mountains, through some of the best settlements and most fertile counties of the State, it is moving still onward, every additional mile signalizing the wisdom which had seized upon what nature had blazed out for a great highway of commerce.

Manufactures.

Fayetteville enjoys the advantage of very considerable water-power, furnished by Cross, Blount's, Rockfish, and Beaver Creeks, running either immediately through the town and its suburbs or the adjacent country. This water-power may be immeasurably increased (the matter has been and is now agitated by the citizens) by the reopening of the old canal, giving an unlimited volume of water, with sufficient fall, from the Cape Fear River, and pursuing a system which has recently achieved such wonderful results at Columbia, S. C. The old canal-bed, some portions nearly intact, can be traced from its beginning, a few miles north of town, through the environs, to the original basin, near the corner of Hay and Winslow Streets, and which the boys fifty years ago used as a skating-pond.

The Fayetteville Cotton Mills, located on the site of the old Mallett factory, only three-fourths of a mile from the business centre of the town, is one of the new manufacturing enterprises of the progressive city. Since the organization of the company, last spring, two dams have been constructed, together with factory building of two stories, forty-eight by one hundred feet, besides picket-house, offices, '&c. All the machinery is of the most improved patterns, purchased direct from the manufacturers, and comprises sixteen self-stripping cards, ten spinning frames, two thousand and eighty spindles, speeders, railway heads, &c.

Commencing with a capital of $32,250, with the privilege of an increase to $100,000, the success of the company has been very gratifying since its organization. The energy of the younger business men of the community has been evoked to guarantee its success, and representative men of all classes of the population have subscribed of their moderate means to the establishment of this important industry in their midst. It is a most satisfactory illustration of what persistent and concerted effort can accomplish upon the basis of a limited capital.

The Bluff Mills, on Beaver Creek, a three-story brick building, with boiler-house, cotton storage warehouse, &c., are run by a sixty-inch turbine wheel, and have three thousand and fifty-six spindles and sixty-two looms; they consume about thirteen hundred and forty pounds of cotton per day. The mills produce thirty-six hundred and twenty-two yards of sheeting daily; the machinery here is also of modern pattern. The mills employ a well-organized army of from one hundred and fifty to one hundred and sixty competent operatives, who, with their dependencies, make up a comfortable town of five hundred or six hundred inhabitants. There are seventeen hundred and thirty-six acres of land and fifty odd tenement-houses belonging to the factories, and two stores supply the hands with the necessaries of life. The mills turn out a fine class of three-yard sheetings and Nos. 7 and 10 yarns; also cotton paddings. The products are very popular; about one-half of them, including all the yarns, are sold in North Carolina. The New York agents are Woodward, Baldwin & Co., and in Baltimore Woodward Baldwin & Norris, through whose hands the "Lake George" and "Lebanon" 4-4 heavy brown sheetings of the Beaver Creek and Bluff Mills find their way throughout the world. A stock of these goods are kept in the store in Fayetteville, where the president has his office.

The Cumberland Mills, situated on Beaver Creek, adjacent to Bluff Mills, comprise the main building of four stories, fifty by one hundred feet; dye-house, thirty by ninety feet; lapper-house, thirty by fifty feet; store-room, twenty by fifty feet. There are eighty-six looms and twenty-eight hundred

HAY STREET, FAYETTEVILLE, N. C.

spindles, run by one hundred and twenty horse-power, and employing one hundred and twenty operatives; they consume twenty-five hundred pounds raw cotton per day, with a total production of twenty-seven hundred pounds goods daily, which consist of fine cottonades, seamless bags, twines and carpet warp. These goods are sold in New York, Philadelphia and Cincinnati. The labor is all native, and, where taken from the country around and taught, not generally satisfactory.

There are, besides, a bucket factory now in successful operation, for the manufacture of well-buckets, pails, tubs, measures and other articles of woodenware, to which the company expect to add the machinery for making spokes, helves and shuttles; one of the largest establishments in the South for the manufacture of turpentine stills (for which they have a lucrative trade all over the Southern country) together with tobacco flues; a factory making turpentine hacks and other tools, which employs a large force and carries on an immense business; a plow manufactory, supplying a large percentage of the farmers of all that region; a clothing manufactory, newly established and giving steady work to forty or fifty hands; a sash, blind and door factory; two wood-turning factories; one iron foundry; the extensive Merchant flour and corn mills; three grist mills; one very complete flour mill (patent roller process); one wool-carding mill; one cotton-seed oil mill (running night and day at the height of the season); one wagon factory; one carriage factory (known as one of the most extensive in the South); one candy factory; two soda and beer bottling establishments; one brick-yard (very extensive)—besides the numerous lumber and planing mills, cooper and blacksmith shops demanded by the large and increasing business of the community.

Other industries are projected, and stock has already been taken for the erection of another cotton mill. Increased interest in the subject of manufacturing is observable in the community, and a realization of the fact that substantial prosperity is proportional with the number and extent of those enterprises which give steady employment to large numbers of people, supply a self-sustaining, thrifty population, utilize the raw material of our varied products, and increase the circulation of ready money with the aggregate monthly wages of toiling thousands.

Here, too, are located the shops of the Cape Fear and Yadkin Valley Railway Company, which, enlarged in dimensions and added to in machinery and force with the increasing needs of the company, now cover a large area of ground and turn out an immense amount of work—comfortable and beautifully finished passenger cars, box and flat cars, &c., constructed under the advantages of little cost and great convenience accruing from the unlimited timber resources developed along the line of road.

MERCANTILE BUSINESS, &c.

The receipts and shipments of cotton (exclusive of factory consumption) and naval stores will aggregate, in value, not less than from $2,000,000 to $2,250,000 per annum—besides those of the other varied products of the country tributary to Fayetteville. The mercantile trade embraces a large scope of territory—much of it fertile and very productive—and the volume of both wholesale and retail business is gratifying and increasing; of the former—in dry goods, staple and heavy groceries, fertilizers, hardware, agricultural implements, &c.—Fayetteville can boast of some of the most extensive houses in the State.

ATTRACTIONS FOR NORTHERN TOURISTS.

Fayetteville is surrounded on all sides by great forests of pine, with a genial and salubrious climate, which is abundantly evidenced by the remarkably low death-rate of the city's population and the unusual average longevity of its inhabitants, and is rarely subjected to extremities of cold, the thermometer during the severest winters hardly ever falling below twenty degrees. Especially is it a pleasant place of sojourn during the spring months, so trying in the far South and still held in the grasp of winter at the extreme North. Here nature bestirs herself and thaws out under the quickening effects of soft winds and a balmy atmosphere, while summer comes on with hesitant footfall to blow into full flower the bursting buds of springtime.

Seekers after health or pleasure alike want the comforts, the conveniences and the luxuries of life, and these are supplied without stint at the new Hotel La Fayette. Spacious rooms, with the best modern furnishing; tasteful parlors and drawing-rooms; broad stair and hall ways; cosy balconies; a delightfully situated dining-room; comfortable offices and billiard tables—all combine to offer the best features of first-rate hotel entertainment. As to the table, there is no appeal from the unerring judgment of the traveling public; and this "autocrat of the (dinner) table," headed by that affable *bon vivant*, the "drummer," sounds everywhere the praises of the kitchen and larder of the Hotel La Fayette.

The town and its suburbs (notably incomparable Haymount) afford many delightful drives and rides, diversified by level roadways, picturesque streams, and bits of exquisite scenery.

CHARACTERISTICS OF THE PEOPLE, &c.

Fayetteville has lost much of the quaint and picturesque in streets and buildings which so charmed the visitor in past years. The iron front and the

ECCLES PARK, FAYETTEVILLE, N. C.

mansard roof have displaced the plain brick wall and flat roof which made up whole blocks of stores, pierced by archways and corridors to the gloomy warehouses in the rear, and reminding one of nothing so much as the architecture of the benign and simple rule of the Missions on the Pacific coast.

The market-house remains almost alone to tell of how they put together and ornamented brick and mortar when this century was young. The illustration conveys better than description an idea of its perfect proportion, grace and symmetry. The town hall surmounts the market proper, and the building occupies a broad plaza at the intersection of the four main business thoroughfares.

But there is much of the old town in the present generation. Clannish, as befits their Scotch-Irish stock, the people are nevertheless open-handed and generous; they are cultured without ostentation, and gifted with the simple refinement of nature. The uprightness and integrity of its men, and the beauty and virtue of its women, fail not yet to uphold the ancient prestige of the venerable town.

MISCELLANEOUS.

The people of Fayetteville have ever been keenly alive to the importance of utilizing to the fullest extent all the educational advantages vouchsafed to them, and in past years some of the best and most thorough high schools of the State have been there located. Though there are still several private schools in different sections of the city, well patronized, as well as a large and flourishing kindergarten, the graded school system now absorbs a large percentage of the children of Fayetteville. The building is situated on Haymount, the western suburb of the town, and, with ten departments and an efficient corps of teachers, offers to the community fine educational facilities. An excellent public library elevates and refines the literary taste of the people, while ten churches for white and colored invite the different denominations to the worship of God.

A merchants' and cotton exchange, with a numerous membership, with ample facilities for handling, weighing, grading and storing cotton, &c., gives compactness and concert of action to the business interests of the community, and ample banking facilities demanded by the increasing mercantile and manufacturing operations are furnished by one State and one National bank.

On the banks of a beautiful stream, Cross Creek, which winds its way with graceful curve through the most beautiful part of the city, crossed here and there by handsome bridges, is Eccles Park, with gaily-painted boats, handsome boat-houses, grounds for croquet and other out-door pastimes. In pleasant weather it is a place of popular resort, and the stream, alive with boating parties, and the lawns thronged with ladies and children, present an attractive and animated scene.

Including all the suburbs which actually merge into the corporate limits, Fayetteville contains a population of about six thousand, though it is credited with much less by the last census.

At the last legislature a charter was obtained for a street-railway, which the extended area of the place renders desirable and expedient.

The Wilson Short Cut, a branch of the Atlantic Coast Line, has its present terminus at this point.

Cape Fear River transportation of freight and passengers by steamer to Wilmington and intermediate points has always been an important factor in the commerce of Fayetteville, and has been the main channel for the receipt of heavy articles of merchandise. The steamers are comfortable, and the voyage of one hundred and twelve miles to Wilmington pleasant. The boating business on the river has recently been almost entirely consolidated into one company.

The rich bottoms of the Cape Fear River produce immense crops of corn and forage, and the land contiguous to Fayetteville—undulating, light, sandy loam, with clay subsoil, and well watered—is well adapted to truck-farming, fruit-raising and the growth of grapes.

A large floral nursery in the suburbs of the city and several fruit nurseries in the adjacent country are among the profitable industries at this point.

About four miles north of Fayetteville is Tokay Vineyard (one hundred and forty-seven acres), one of the largest, and certainly, in the number of varieties of grapes and other fruit cultivated, the most interesting, east of the Rocky Mountains. Here the Scuppernong, very luxuriant of growth and prolific of yield, occupies many acres of the vineyard; the remainder of the area is devoted to the cultivation of the different trellised table grapes and other fruits—peaches, pears, melons, &c. Ample cellarage, presses, gas-house, storehouses, &c., render Tokay Vineyard complete in every respect; while the elegant mansion of the proprietor, grounds beautifully laid off and adorned with statuary, pleasant walks and drives, make it one of the "show places" of the State, which the Fayetteville people take a pride in showing to the stranger. The vintage of Tokay amounts to about forty thousand or fifty thousand gallons of wine per annum- Scuppernong, Concord, Delaware, &c.—besides which great quantities of table grapes are shipped abroad.

HOPE MILLS No. 2, NEARING COMPLETION.

Southern Division.

FAYETTEVILLE TO BENNETTSVILLE, S. C.—FIFTY-SEVEN MILES.

THE completion of the Southern Division of the Cape Fear and Yadkin Valley Railway, a little more than four years since, has been attended by very beneficent results, not only in the largely increased traffic enjoyed by the road, but in a still greater measure by the opening out and development of a country especially rich in agricultural and forestry resources.

This division traverses Cumberland, Robeson and Richmond counties in this State, and Marlboro county, S. C., to Bennettsville, a distance of fifty-seven miles, and places accessible to market one billion three hundred and fifty million feet of yellow-heart long-leaf pine, besides almost inexhaustible supplies of maple, poplar, juniper, cypress and other useful woods.

After leaving the sand-hills and Big Rockfish, a few miles out from Fayetteville, the traveler surveys a fine farming country clear on to Bennettsville, yielding excellent crops of corn, sorghum and cotton, with a thrifty population, mostly of Scotch-Irish extraction (in the North Carolina counties), and quick to seize upon all the advantages and opportunities vouchsafed to them.

A great impetus has been given to the production of naval stores by this southern extension, and the cutting of timber and sawing of lumber have grown into a business of vast extent. The puffing engines of the mills meet one at every station, and the forests resound, as the train speeds along, with the axe of the woodman. Timber trains are frequently carried into Fayetteville requiring the pulling power of two large engines, and the freight-books of the company show that the business is steadily increasing. It is a gratifying fact, as showing the general thrift and prosperity of the State, that comparatively little of this lumber is shipped out of North Carolina—all the orders coming to the millers that they can possibly fill from nearer home, the Piedmont section constituting a very large and important customer.

HOPE MILLS.

At the first station, seven miles from Fayetteville, are situated the large factories of the Hope Mills Manufacturing Company, of which is appended the following description:—

No. 1 mill, brick building, two hundred and eighty-five feet by fifty feet; one-half two stories, and one-half three stories high. Dye-house one hundred and ten feet by thirty feet; modern machinery. Dry-house twenty feet by thirty feet; modern machinery. Spreader-room and machine-shop, thirty feet by sixty-six feet; two stories.

Mill fitted up with Kitson compound spreaders, twenty-eight roller cards and railroad heads, six drawing frames (American make), two slubber and five fly frames (Higgins' make), fifty-six hundred Excelsior spinning spindles, spoolers and reels, circular warper, one Denn double-head double-linker electric-stop warper, six twisters and four beaming machines, one hundred and ninety box looms—twenty-two of these are sixteen harness. All the machinery is in first-class condition. Goods made—cottonades and cheviots. Help good and well-behaved.

The company have fifty houses in No. 1 village, also saw-mill and store. The village contains two churches and one schoolhouse.

Mill is fitted up with Grennell sprinklers and first-class fire-pump, and is run entirely by water, of which there is a full supply.

Hope Mills No. 2, situated about a mile and a half south of No. 1 village, is an entirely new mill and village, all built within the last twelve months. The mill is three hundred and forty-six feet long by sixty feet wide, two stories high, and is filled with the very latest improved machinery. It will be run entirely by water, of which there is an abundance.

The spreader-room will contain one cotton opener and preparer and four loppers (Potter & Atherton's), card-room, twenty revolving flat cards (Platte's, English make), Howard & Bullock electric-stop drawing frames (Providence machine), a slubber and fly frames.

The spinning-room contains nine thousand Whitin's gravity spindles, Hopedale upright spoolers, Denn's double-head electric-stop warper.

The weave-room contains Wood's reels, winders, and beaming frames, and Knowles' looms. Shafting, hangers and pulleys furnished by W. Sellers & Co., Philadelphia, and water-wheel by the Holyoke Company.

This mill will be lighted by electricity, and is also fitted up with the Grennell fire system. Also has powerful pump with outside hydrants. It is now about ready to operate; will manufacture fine yarns and fine ginghams. The structure is built of brick.

The village contains sixty well-built houses, all nicely painted. The water is first rate, and the location healthy.

The capital of the Hope Mills Manufacturing Company is $300,000.

RED SPRINGS.

No point on the line of the road can show a more rapid growth, with a consequent increase in population, business and industries, than this thriv-

TURNPIKE BRIDGE, LYNDON, VT.

ing village. Five years since Red Springs was a little settlement in the woods; now it is a fair town on the highway of railway travel, with several stores, two hotels, an excellent newspaper, mills, cooper and blacksmith shops, &c. Then the inmates of one or two families made up the sum of its inhabitants; now it numbers its population by the hundreds, with church and school facilities rarely enjoyed by a place of its size.

There are ten saw and planing mills, including a sash, blind and door factory within the limits of the corporation or in the immediate vicinity, which together employ over two hundred and forty hands (representing, with the average *per capita* of families, a population of about one thousand, supported by these industries), and pay out from $700 to $800 per week in wages.

Private enterprise has also here built a narrow-gauge railroad through the heart of the pine forest, for the saving of time, labor and money in hauling the logs to the mills, and it has also been eagerly utilized by the farmers of the vicinity in getting their products to market.

Red Springs derives its name from that which invested it with interest and importance among the people of this section of the State long before the days of railroads: its chalybeate springs of iron in solution, very highly charged, magnesia and sulphur. Their medicinal virtues have been thoroughly tested and long known, and the increase of visitors to enjoy for the season the healthful waters of these exhaustless fountains is notable every year. The springs (of which there are two) are unlimited in supply, and apparently have no bottom, for the "longest pole" in all the country around has never yet succeeded in making "soundings."

MAXTON.

Prior to the change of its name on application of its citizens, this place rejoiced in the curious appellation of Shoe Heel. This, we may reasonably infer, from the Scotch element predominating so largely in Robeson county, was a corruption of Quhele, a clan exterminated in pitched battle by the Clan Chattan during the reign of Robert of Scotland, and immortalized in Scott's romance of the "Fair Maid of Perth." Maxton is a flourishing town, and is destined to acquire additional importance from its favored position as the trade centre of the rich agricultural communities of Richmond and Robeson counties, and a considerable scope of country in South Carolina. The shipments of naval stores and cotton are very large, and the business of general merchandising is steadily on the increase.

Maxton is an unusually intelligent community, marked by great refinement in its social circle, and enjoys exceptional religious and educational advantages.

The population is now about seven hundred, the rate of increase being very great within the past four years. It is at the intersection of the Cape Fear and Yadkin Valley and Carolina Central Railways.

BENNETTSVILLE.

Bennettsville is the county-seat of Marlboro, S. C., one of the best cotton-producing counties in the State, ranking second in the amount of its annual crop. The land almost verifies the description of "level as a floor," and farming is done still on almost the grand scale of the days prior to the war. The planters "pitch" for big crops and fertilize extensively even the naturally rich soil of heavy loam subsoiled with clay. A part of the county furnishes excellent grazing, abundantly evidenced by the number of fine cattle, farm horses and mules, and blooded stock for riding and driving.

Bennettsville, since the completion of the road in December, 1884, has enjoyed exceptional prosperity. An industrious population has been attracted thither for the purpose of engaging in mercantile business, rendered profitable by the impetus given to agriculture, to invest in property or engage in industrial enterprises. The people are proud of their town, and are admirably sustained in this feeling by a good municipal government. They are liberal supporters of churches and schools, of which the consequence is a moral and law-abiding community.

A prosperous banking establishment meets the needs of this enterprising business community, and a charter has been obtained for the establishment of a cotton factory.

The court-house is a very fine structure, of unique but attractive style of architecture, occupying the centre of a spacious square fronting the business part of the town, with an interior admirably arranged and fitted up.

The contemplated extension of the Southern Division of the Cape Fear and Yadkin Valley Railway to Camden Junction offers comparatively few difficulties in engineering after bridging and crossing the Pee Dee, will increase the tributary area of rich farming territory, and will furnish important railroad connection with lines running south, via the Three C's, South Carolina and Wilmington and Columbia Railroads.

INTERMEDIATE STATIONS.

Lumber Bridge, McNatt's, Shandon, Wakulla, Floral College, John's, Hasty, McColl's, and Tatum's are all busy and important stations on the line of the Southern Division, plying a brisk trade in general country merchandise, and making large shipments of cotton, naval stores, timber, lumber, &c. In the cotton season the freight receipts on this part of the road

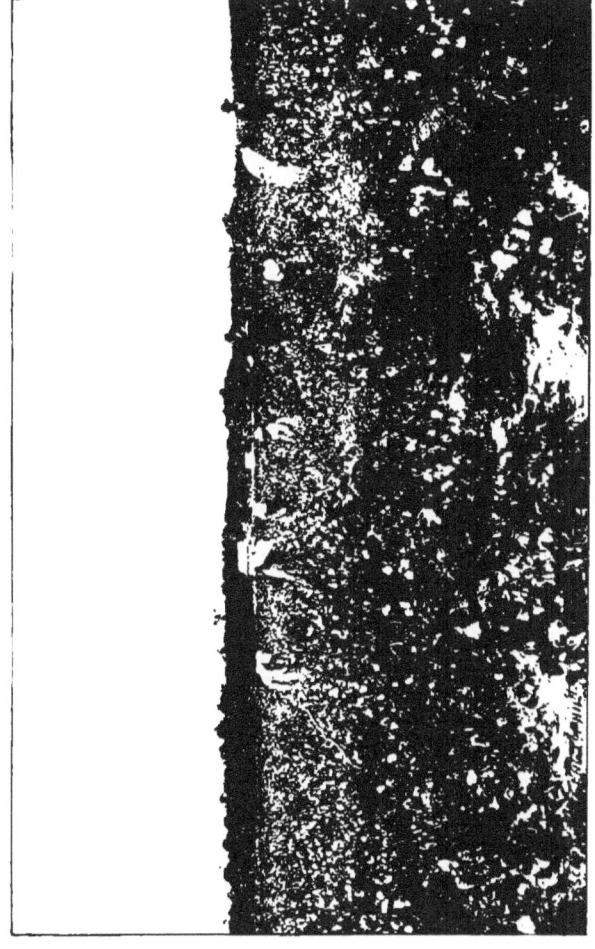

COTTON FIELD ABOUT FLORAL COLLEGE, N. C.

necessitate all the dispatch possible in moving the crop, and frequently tax the rolling stock to its full capacity. Exclusive of Wilmington, Bennettsville ranks third among the stations on the Cape Fear and Yadkin Valley as a shipping point.

Fayetteville is now enjoying a splendid trade from this Southern Division. The merchants of Lumber Bridge, McNatt's, Shandon, John's and the other stations above mentioned in South Carolina are prompt-paying and valuable customers for large orders in dry goods, staple groceries, fertilizers and general merchandise. Even in the former days of inland and wagon trade, the business of Fayetteville, gathered from Robeson, Richmond and South Carolina, was more profitable than that of the western country, as the cotton brought to market by the farmers and planters of that section always commanded ready money, while the western commodities—hides, tallow, butter, flaxseed and other grain—were exchanged, in barter, for the articles carried back for home consumption.

Few persons would recognize the city of to-day with the town of ten years ago. One side of Person Street has been almost entirely rebuilt with fine brick edifices, while Hay Street is a picture of architectural beauty, from Donaldson Street to Market Square. The taste of the householder and real estate owner has kept pace with this business enterprise, and the suburbs are beautified by many elegant and tasteful residences.

COURT-HOUSE, GREENSBORO, N. C.

Upper Cape Fear and Deep River Division.

FROM FAYETTEVILLE TO GREENSBORO—NINETY-SEVEN MILES.

HIS division leads through the counties of Cumberland, Harnett, Moore, Chatham, Randolph and Guilford to Greensboro, at the junction of the North Carolina Railroad with the Richmond and Danville. The hill country now succeeds with the route of the line inland, and very rapidly after leaving Gulf, an altitude being reached at Greensboro, eight hundred and fifty feet above sea level, about seven hundred and fifty feet higher than that at Fayetteville, more than two-thirds of which elevation is attained in a distance of fifty miles.

Fayetteville is the centre of a large extent of country, embracing part of Cumberland, the counties of Robeson and Richmond on the south and southwest, and Moore and Harnett on the west and northwest, which has been for many years one of the great naval-stores-producing sections of the South, and Fayetteville was second only to Wilmington in the exportation of this great commercial staple. At one time there might be counted in the environs of the city twenty-eight turpentine distilleries, working on full time throughout the season. With the lapse of years much of the virgin pine has of course been boxed, but vast tracts of uncut long-leaf still lie in easy access of the road. Similar in some, but not in all respects, to the soil of the Southern and Eastern Divisions, the light loams and clayey loams of the upper Cape Fear continue for about one-third of the distance embraced in this division, after which the country changes entirely in soil, topography and geological formation. The gray soil intermixed with gravel, and the red and dark-colored soils of the region of slate and granite, appear. The country is broken and rugged, and on all sides crop out evidences of the existence of extensive and valuable mineral deposits; the long-leaf pine disappears, and the oak forests supervene, very fine bodies of which extend along Deep River, and on both sides of the railway line to Greensboro. Walnut, hickory and dogwood also abound along the route, extensive shipments of which are being made by different individuals and companies.

MINERALS.

Mention has already been made of the coal mines of this region, and the matter will be more specifically treated farther on. As to the quality of the coal, the highest geological authority has pronounced it "well adapted for fuel, cooking, gas, and oil. It is a shining, clear coal, resembling the best specimens of Cumberland. It ignites easily, burns with a bright, clear combustion, and leaves a very light purplish-gray ash. It swells and agglutinates, making a hollow fire. It yields a shining and very porous coke, and is an excellent coal for making gas or for burning." (Report of Admiral Wilkes to the Secretary of the Navy.) Lying along these coal beds are deposits of ball-iron ore, as well as other ore beds along the line of railway or in the vicinity within an area of twenty by forty miles. A geological report of Professor Emmons gives the general character of these ores:—

Sesquioxide of iron	69.73	67.50
Protoxide of iron	0.84	47.50
Phosphoric acid	.06	
Sulphur	.09	3.39
Carbon	31.30	34.00

But of all the mineral deposits of this region the most valuable ore bed is found at Ore Hill. The veins seem to be without limit, several being from fifteen to eighteen feet in thickness. Many of these veins have been opened and worked at various times, producing mainly limonite ore. It makes an excellent, tough iron, being porous and easily smelted. From samples selected by the late Professor Kerr, State Geologist, out of a heap of several hundred tons, the following analyses are by Genth and Hanna:—

Silica	1.42	3.79
Oxide of iron	82.02	83.80
Lime and magnesia	1.30	
Phosphorus	.00	
Sulphur	.00	.44

Professor Kerr says: "The purity of this ore is conspicuous, and the quantity seems to be very great."

Lying some distance farther up Deep River are outcropping beds of magnetic, and, in one or two instances, specular, iron ore, which during the civil war were worked with gratifying results, producing iron of superior quality.

Between Sanford and Egypt red and gray sandstone, and a little farther west granite, exist in large quantities. These stones are already being quarried, and their demand for building purposes will steadily increase with the present facilities of transportation and the rapid progress of the country.

In Moore county a very superior quality of mill stone is found in immense strata, both on upper Little River and at the extensive works of Parkewood, on

GREENSBORO FEMALE COLLEGE, GREENSBORO, N. C.

Deep River, and "Moore County grit" is, without exaggeration, favorably known the whole country over.

Soapstone is found at various points in the upper part of Moore and along the line of Chatham counties. These beds were successfully worked years ago, and constituted a profitable industry to that section. The demand for soapstone in the great markets of the world is practically limitless; and, accessible as the railway has now made these quarries, we may expect them to be soon again in active operation. A bed of soapstone, which promises to be quite valuable, has recently been discovered in Guilford county.

Capital seeking investment will gradually realize the value of the gold mines of Moore and Randolph, which, imperfectly worked before the war without the present improved mechanical appliances, yielded in many cases very satisfactory returns.

WATER-POWER.

A recently published descriptive gazette of the Cape Fear and Yadkin Valley Railway says of the manufacturing enterprises located upon Deep River: "The Deep River factories, so located that a common terminal point will place the most remote within four miles of the branch line, are the Franklinville, Cedar Falls, Randolph, J. M. Worth, Randleman, Naomi, Columbia, Central Falls, and Enterprise Manufacturing Companies—nine mills, twenty-four thousand six hundred and sixty-eight spindles, six hundred and ninety-six looms, ninety-one carders, employing twelve hundred operatives, consuming seventeen thousand pounds of raw cotton per day, and freighting in and out thirty-seven thousand pounds of raw material, supplies, merchandise and manufactured goods daily. These factories feed and clothe four thousand persons." A competent authority has estimated the full water-power of Deep River at nine hundred and fifty thousand spindles, and of the Cape Fear River, above Fayetteville, at two million, making a total of three million spindles, all within the scope of less than eighty miles of the road, embraced entirely in the Upper Cape Fear and Deep River Division.

The Deep River factories, since the date of the above estimate, exhibit a very gratifying increase in the value of plants and machinery, extent of operations, output of goods, &c. The number of mills remains the same, a new factory having been erected and one removed to another point on the line of road. The looms have been increased from six hundred and ninety-six to one thousand and twenty-eight, the carders to over one hundred, while there has been an addition of about fifteen per cent. to the force of employés. The freighting in and out of raw material, &c., has advanced from thirty-seven thousand to about fifty thousand pounds daily, with a corresponding augmentation of raw cotton consumed. All the mills are supplied with the latest improvements, and nearly all lighted by electricity.

AGRICULTURAL PRODUCTS.

The farm products of this division are varied and important, and comprise cotton, corn, oats, wheat, rye, sorghum cane, Irish and sweet potatoes, fine cabbage, onions, &c., &c.

MANCHESTER MILLS.

At the first station west of Fayetteville are the Manchester Mills, occupying a building two hundred and twenty-five by forty feet, and running nineteen hundred spindles and fifty-five plaid looms. The mills manufacture plaids and stripes, which are sold all over North and South Carolina and Virginia. There is a forty horse-power of water with a sixty horse-power engine.

McFADYEN SPRINGS.

In the vicinity of Manchester, lying upon Little River, are the McFadyen Springs, enjoying a very enviable reputation in all the adjacent country for the remarkable medicinal efficacy of their waters in the cure of cutaneous and scrofulous diseases, and the alleviation of all liver complaints and ailments growing out of dyspepsia and disordered stomach. So strongly impregnated are these waters with the chemical constituents which make up their analysis that the wet earth at the bottom of the spring and on its sides is used with wonderful effect as a plaster in eruptions, sores, &c. The McFadyen Springs have been little advertised; and, even with the present railroad facilities, no effort has been made to bring them into public notice. The accommodations are very rude and primitive—simply a few cabins, which are used by Fayetteville families and those in the vicinity; but in coming years McFadyen Springs will doubtless attain the prominence which they deserve.

Spout Spring and Swann's Stations are thriving points on the line, the former the centre of a great lumber milling business, and the latter making large shipments of naval stores.

JONESBORO.

The traveler greets this gladly as one of the most attractive towns on the line of the Cape Fear and Yadkin Valley Railway, presenting an appearance of thrift and prosperity, with its neat residences, numerous stores and church spires and school belfries, which is very inviting. Long established

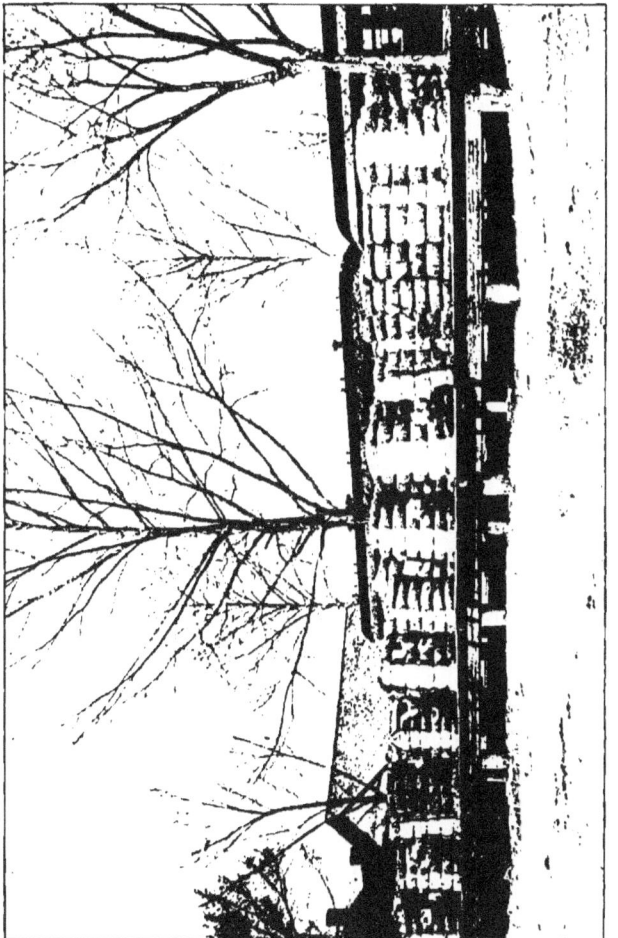

COTTON PLATFORM, JONESBORO, N. C.

as a trading point for a prosperous section, Jonesboro has of late years become quite an important cotton market, receiving and shipping large quantities of the staple every season. The cultivation of bright yellow leaf tobacco has also been largely entered into by the farmers of Moore county, which the progressive spirit of the place has met by the erection of two commodious tobacco warehouses.

A few weeks ago a very important forward step was taken in manufacturing by enterprising citizens of the community, by the establishment of a cotton mill, with complete plant, improved machinery, &c., for the manufacture of yarns and carpet fillings.

There is a banking establishment to meet mercantile and other demands, wagon and buggy factory, a good newspaper, with many other adjuncts of a flourishing community. The people are moral and law-abiding, and pay special attention to the support of their churches and schools.

SANFORD.

Sanford is at the intersection of the Cape Fear and Yadkin Valley and Raleigh and Augusta Air-Line Railroads, whence connection is made with Charlotte, Wilmington, and Raleigh. The town draws a lucrative trade from the rich farming segments of three counties lying in a corner, and has, besides, sash and door factory, marble works, and several other remunerative industries. It enjoys also the advantage of a well-established and excellently-edited newspaper. In the vicinity is a quarry of excellent brownstone, already successfully worked.

THE EGYPT COAL MINES.

The Egypt Coal Company, which purchased the Egypt mine estate—comprising twelve hundred acres of coal land, twelve hundred acres of timber land, and three hundred acres in a high state of cultivation—have, at the date of this publication, very nearly restored the machine plant and accomplished the unwatering of the mine, the shaft of which is four hundred and sixty-three feet in depth, with twelve hundred feet of gangway, numerous slopes, chambers, &c. The machinery has been put in excellent repair, pit-head erected and all the timbering restored; the steam used in the operation of the machinery has been produced from refuse coal lying upon the dump for over twenty years—a remarkably strong proof of its excellent quality—and, to guard against every possible contingency, the company have laid a pipe line one-fourth of a mile in length from a spring which will furnish an ample supply of water.

The present machine plant and the openings in the mine have a capacity of about three hundred tons per day, and the company anticipate no difficulty in mining and marketing an output of that amount within the State. The property, prior to its coming into the hands of the present management, represented a cash capital of $250,000 for machinery, developments and improvements, and the additional outlay with the present company has already reached into the thousands. Hitherto, operations have been conducted under great disadvantage, and at expense for labor and material far in excess of what the same now costs—changed conditions by which the present company will undoubtedly profit. A branch line of railway a mile long, extending from Egypt Depot to the shaft of the mine, has been graded and cross-ties delivered, so that the work will be completed by the time the mining company is ready to ship coal.

A brownstone quarry of approved quality has also been opened, and when fully uncovered the shipments of its excellent building material will doubtless be much increased.

An extensive saw-mill has been erected on the company's property, and a brick-yard will soon be in operation.

A town site—Egypt Depot—has been laid off, and an architect has drawn plans for several buildings which will be erected forthwith.

Gulf, Goldston, Richmond and Ore Hill are the next four stations west from Egypt, all showing a steady and gratifying increase in business and population each year.

Near Ore Hill are the

MOUNT VERNON SPRINGS,

whose waters have been carefully analyzed, and undoubtedly possess unusual medicinal efficacy. They have become a popular summer resort, and, with contemplated enlarged and improved hotel accommodations, will continue to attract numbers of visitors.

SILER CITY.

Siler City, having tributary to it an excellent agricultural section, has grown rapidly, and has been quick to seize upon the opportunities presented by railway communication with the outside world, in bending every effort to build up its business in merchandise, and enhance the value of its industrial pursuits. Here is located a good boarding and day school, under the management and supervision of careful and efficient instructors, and offering the advantages of excellent physical, mental and moral training.

Siler City has a large tobacco warehouse, several lumber and planing mills, together with a number of prosperous and energetic business houses and men. A gratifying evidence of the growth and thrift of the surrounding country is found in the success attending the exhibitions of the annual agricultural fair held at Siler City.

WATER TOWER, GREENSBORO, N. C.

STALEY.

This busy place has literally sprung into existence with the westward extension of the road. Emerging from the woods with the advent of steam and the flying train, its growth has been lusty and its prosperity remarkable. Its population is about two hundred, with nine stores, shuttle factory, chair factory, saw mills and planing mills within its limits and in the immediate vicinity. It never fails to make an excellent exhibit on the freight-books of the company, as it is one of the shipping points of the Deep River Cotton Mills, and its merchants carry on a brisk trade in the shipment of poultry and other farm products, while they deal largely in furs and dried fruits.

The lands of this section and on to Liberty produce a very fine grade of bright yellow leaf tobacco, growing also some of the finest fruits of different varieties raised throughout the extent of the line.

LIBERTY.

Liberty is beautifully situated, and presents a very pleasing appearance to the incoming railway passenger. The extension of its limits and the growth of its population have been very marked within the past two or three years, and the citizens now claim a total of between five hundred and six hundred inhabitants. An act of incorporation has been recently granted by the legislature, and many contemplated and actual improvements evince the spirit of progress and enterprise. A fine school is established here, which, for discipline, efficiency and curriculum of study, has already taken high rank among the educational institutions of that section. A large area of country surrounding Liberty is admirably adapted to sheep husbandry. The land is well drained, high and dry, offering fine ranges for flocks. The mutton raised is not very large but of excellent quality, and the wool clip is good.

Julian, Factory Junction (from which extends the Millboro Branch, connecting with the factories at Deep River) and Pleasant Garden are the last three stations on the road leading into Greensboro.

GREENSBORO.

Greensboro, the beautiful gateway into the fair Piedmont region, merits with emphasis the importance given it as a great "railroad centre:"—the point of junction of the Cape Fear and Yadkin Valley and Richmond and Danville Railroads, with the various extensive connections of both systems, which embrace the main and branch lines leading south and southeast to Wilmington, Bennettsville and Fayetteville; north to Danville, Richmond,

Washington and beyond; east to Raleigh, Goldsboro and New Berne; southwest to Salisbury, Asheville and Charlotte; west to Madison, Winston, Salem and Mt. Airy. Twenty-two passenger trains arrive at and depart from the depots of the city during the twenty-four hours; and, as the time-tables of a large part of these include only the hours of morning from 8 to 10 A. M., and evening from 8 to 11 P. M., the stir and bustle of moving baggage-trucks, hurrying passengers, crowded waiting-rooms, rattling omnibuses, hacks, &c., give the traveler a pleasing impression of the progressive life of the city, which a walk through its crowded thoroughfares and along its blocks of handsome business houses will confirm and strengthen.

Not through accident has Greensboro attained its present prominence on the highway of railway travel. For more than half a century its leading citizens—among whom were men entrusted, by virtue of their commanding abilities and high character, with the most weighty public responsibilities, the helm of State government and high place in its councils—have been ever keenly alive to the material advancement of the people through great measures of internal improvement, devoting their energies, time and money not only to the development of the Cape Fear and Yadkin Valley. Railway system, but to the promotion and completion of other important roads in North Carolina. Those who have come after them have not been careless of the example or unworthy of the trust committed to their hands, and active in the business circles of the town to-day are men who have done a giant's work in weaving about it the network of steel rails which gives it profitable traffic and smiling prosperity.

The City's Growth.

The fine surrounding farming country and its many other natural advantages would never permit Greensboro to stagnate or languish; consequently its whole history is that of one of the thrifty, flourishing places of the State. But its growth within a decade has been very marked; its progress during the past five years has been especially gratifying, since the completion of the Cape Fear and Yadkin Valley Railway in 1884. The compact area enclosing the city proper, and finding its centre in the public square containing the court-house and United States Government building, has proven inadequate to the needs both of business men and householders; and the extension of the suburbs—beautified by tasteful residences and neat cottages, and enlivened by machine-shops and other industrial establishments—has been constant and rapid. It is not extravagant to say that the growth of the suburb of South Greensboro has been phenomenal. Five years have trans-

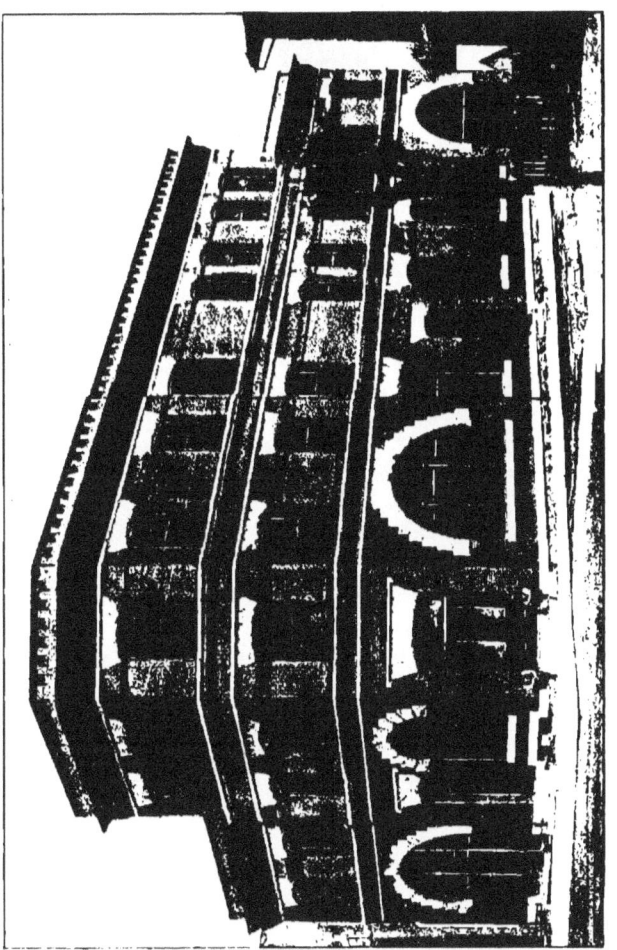

NATIONAL BANK OF GREENSBORO, N. C.

formed it from a straggling settlement into a town of itself, with comfortable and elegant abodes, artistic flower yards and grounds, and beautiful streets.

An estimate of population must of course be approximate, but that the increase has been great is beyond question. Including extensive environs south, southwest, west, and east, a careful computation, based on the number of new buildings erected, the increased volume of business, and the largely-augmented vote at the last election of the two townships in which the town is comprised, would give Greensboro a place in the next census of not far from seven thousand inhabitants. This includes all the suburbs which have hitherto had no place in the count of the population.

Public Works and Improvements.

Nature's generosity and man's energy having made Greensboro a city, its people have resolved that it should have the garniture, furnishing and conveniences of a city, and for the past few years the work of improvement has been systematic and steady.

The fall of 1888 saw the completion of an extensive system of water-works, of the combined standpipe and direct pressure form, with about three miles of main pipe, fifty public and three private fire-hydrants, the tower being located in the vicinity of the railway depots—a prominent and imposing object which catches the eye of the traveler miles away. An ample supply of water is furnished for the manifold uses of the community, and for the most serious emergencies of fire.

Sidewalks have been laid of Fayetteville brick, of very excellent and lasting material, the roadway paved with granite blocks quarried at Flat Rock, near Mt. Airy; and Elm Street, the main business thoroughfare, presents a handsome and attractive appearance throughout.

The fire department is excellent, the citizens universally giving it their cordial co-operation and support, with a full realization of its importance. A commodious and well-arranged building accommodates the steam fire-engine and hook and ladder truck, with the horses in training, and the quarters of the supervising night watchman. The department includes hose-reel teams, conveniently located in different quarters of the city, and other improvements are in contemplation—the putting in of an electric fire-alarm, &c.

The city is lighted by both gas and electricity, and few places in the South can claim a better or more effective system, taking in not only the business streets but those ramifying out into the remote suburbs.

Manufactures.

There are now, within the city proper, or comprised in the limits of its different suburbs:—

- 3 iron foundries, making plows, turbine and other wheels, ironware, castings, &c., &c.
- 2 sash, blind and door factories—one very extensive in its operations, just fitted out with new machinery, demanding immense supplies of raw material, and turning out a large amount of first-class work, which is shipped by all the railroad lines to different points.
- 3 manufactories of plug tobacco.
- 1 cigar factory.
- 2 wagon factories.
- 1 carriage and buggy factory.
- 2 shoe factories.
- 1 large merchant flour and grain mill (with another in course of completion).
- 1 ice factory.
- 1 spoke and handle factory.
- 1 steam beer-bottling establishment.
- Electric-light plant.
- Gas-works.
- 1 mattress factory.
- 1 terra cotta factory.
- 4 brick yards.
- 2 manufactories of tinware.
- 1 manufactory of Tar Heel Liniment.

Throughout the country adjacent the fruit and vegetable canning industry has assumed important proportions, with every indication of future remunerative returns.

It will be seen that, in comparison with its wealth, influence and importance, Greensboro's manufacturing interests are in their infancy. This condition of things will not endure long. Outside capital will be attracted hither by the unparalleled advantages offered; enterprise and public spirit at home will speedily utilize all the means available; cotton and woolen mills will follow the wood-works, these to be supplemented by the furnace and the foundry.

Mercantile Business, &c.

The rapid building up of South Elm Street, as the demands of trade passed the bounds of East and West Market, as well as the lively traffic now daily seen on South Davie Street, are gratifying evidences of the annually increasing business in all the branches of merchandise. Besides the local trade which a tributary productive territory must throw into the hands of its merchants, Greensboro's unrivaled facilities cannot fail to make it the *entrepot*

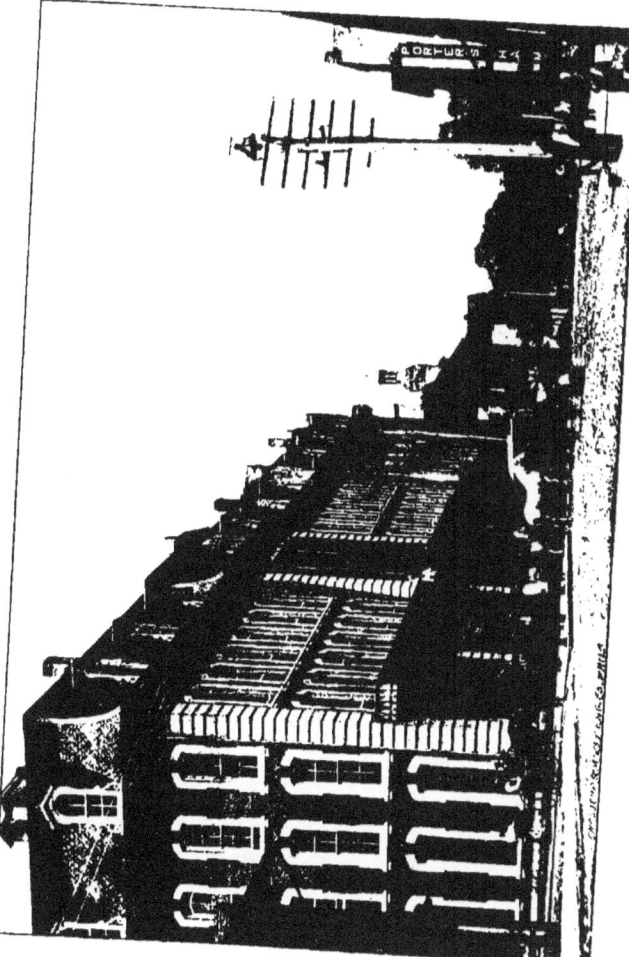

SOUTH ELM STREET, GREENSBORO, N.C.

for a large surrounding area of country accessible by rail, and the future will continue to swell the volume of its wholesale and retail business in dry goods, groceries, hardware, ironware, agricultural implements, sash, doors, blinds and other building material, &c., &c. Facts are more satisfactory than generalities, and statistical information, carefully gathered from time to time, shows that the aggregate of merchandise purchases of the city has increased nearly fifty per cent. in the past three years.

The trade in dried fruits of this market is enormous, and includes apples, peaches, pears, cherries and the different berries. Great improvement has been made by the growers in the drying and treatment of fruits, and the goods shipped from this point obtain a high rating in the Northern markets. The fruit is reckoned, not by bushels, one may say, but by immense bins and great car-loads, forty of the latter in dried apples alone being shipped by one firm last season. This business is of some months' duration—from late spring until autumn—and gives employment to hundreds in picking, drying and marketing.

Such a business community demands proportional monetary and financial facilities, and these are furnished by three banks, exclusive of the savings and deposit institution, one of which (the National Bank of Greensboro) showed, during the twelve months of 1888, average daily deposits of $15,221.64, and average daily checks paid $15,302.55, making it safe to place the total volume of the bank's transactions at $40,000 per day.

BUSINESS ORGANIZATION.

The mercantile circles of the city are unified and incited to concert of action by the Chamber of Commerce, which embraces in its membership the leading and influential citizens of the place, whose efforts as an organized body have already been potent in advancing the general welfare, and the Chamber will not fail of the accomplishment of much good with the city's future growth.

The Land and Improvement Company has been recently established, with the object, primarily, of pushing the trade in leaf tobacco by the erection of suitable buildings; it will also prove useful in systematizing the sales of real estate, placing investments, &c.

TOBACCO INTERESTS.

The tobacco business is in the hands of pushing, aggressive men, who do not suffer it to flag, and finds its facilities for marketing, sales, handling of the leaf and manufacture in three large sales warehouses, nine prize factories, three plug and twist manufactories, and one cigar factory (the latter four already mentioned under the heading of "manufactures"). The city's rightful place as an important tobacco market has not hitherto been fully appreciated, or, rather, fully utilized; but strenuous efforts have of late been made to accomplish this, with substantial results. The compiler is permitted to take from the last annual report of Julius A. Gray, president of the Chamber of Commerce, the following figures:—

"The leaf tobacco sold on this market from October, 1887, to October, 1888, aggregates.................................... 2,276,173 lbs.
That purchased by our dealers on other markets during the same period.. 792,311 lbs.

Making the total handled by Greensboro tobacconists........ 3,068,484 lbs."

The above creditable exhibit is dwarfed by the developments of the present season. Such has been the impetus given to the Greensboro tobacco business that a good crop year would have increased these figures by at least one-half. Within the past three years the number of prize-houses has risen from three to nine, with a corresponding forward movement in the manufacture of the leaf. The warehouses are selling tobacco from the twelve counties of Guilford, Surry, Stokes, Forsyth, Davie, Davidson, Randolph, Chatham, Orange, Alamance, Caswell and Rockingham, besides large and frequent shipments to them from Tennessee, Virginia and South Carolina. No market in the State has access by rail and wagon to a larger and more productive area of the "Bright Tobacco Belt," and this, with its unexcelled shipping facilities and advantages of transportation to all outside markets, must eventually place Greensboro abreast of the foremost tobacco towns of the South.

School Advantages.

These are exceptionally fine, and will be examined with satisfaction by all contemplating investment in property and a permanent residence among the people of this favored community. The White graded school of the city proper has an enrollment of about four hundred and thirty, with an average daily attendance of three hundred and thirty-five pupils, with efficient superintendence, complete departments in the different educational branches, and a full corps of teachers. Bellevue Academy, in South Greensboro, offers the same facilities to the children of that part of the city.

Greensboro Female College, occupying an imposing structure in the centre of beautiful and spacious grounds at the head of West Market Street, is the

WHITE GRADED SCHOOL, GREENSBORO, N. C.

denominational high school of the Methodist Episcopal Church South in North Carolina, and enjoys a wide area of patronage throughout the South. The course of study is thorough, with painstaking preparations in fitting feminine accomplishments, and the discipline wise and effective, making the institution well deserve its high character and enviable popularity. There are, besides, several good private schools; and it will not be amiss to note here that county and town are worthy of each other, for Guilford probably contains more long-established, well-sustained schools within its borders than any other county in the State.

PUBLIC BUILDINGS.

If not in the number, certainly in the attractive architecture and artistic finish, of its public buildings, Greensboro may invite comparison with other towns of its wealth, size and population. The graded school building, in North Greensboro, is graceful and elegant in style, with an interior admirably fitted and arranged for its purposes, and an oratorium for musical, dramatic or literary entertainments.

The county court-house is a model for buildings of the kind. The architect succeeded in blending the durable and ornamental with unusual taste and skill, and presented to the people of the county a piece of work well worthy the expenditure of money required.

The Government building occupies a very eligible location on South Elm Street—a massive and ornate piece of architecture. It contains the post-office and the offices of the Federal Government.

The National Bank of Greensboro has just completed a new building at the corner of South Elm and East Washington Streets. It is of brick, with granite facings, cornice and other exterior work, while the interior is finished in beautiful native dressed pine, with an unusual completeness of arrangement in vault, banking-room, president's and directors' rooms, &c. Two handsome stores also form parts of this commodious structure. The second story has been specially arranged for and is rented for a term of years to the Young Men's Club of Greensboro and the Chamber of Commerce, and the third story has been arranged for and rented for a term of years to the Masonic Lodge of Greensboro.

A PLEASANT PLACE OF SOJOURN.

A climate never approaching the severity of the North in winter and particularly delightful in summer, a healthfulness unquestioned, and freedom from the virulence of malarial diseases, enable Greensboro to offer no mean attractions to the delicate invalid or the pleasure-seeking tourist. Especially during the months of May, June, July and August is it a charming abiding-place. Within two or three hours' ride of the matchless scenery of the Piedmont and Blue Ridge country, and the chalybeate, sulphur and alum springs which make that section celebrated, while but little farther in point of time and distance from the pleasures of Carolina Beach and Wrightsville Sound, the Northern traveler may rest here as his "point of vantage," to seek "green fields and pastures new" in a day's jaunt or a week's journeying in any direction.

The Benbow and McAdoo Houses furnish first-rate hotel accommodations, combining all the conveniences, comforts and luxuries of table, room and attendance which the experienced voyager demands and expects in these enlightened days. So well known is the excellent character of the entertainment afforded by them that the city has long been the Sunday stopping-place of the traveling salesman, who puts no more important question to himself on the eve of one of his rare periods of rest than Falstaff's query: "Shall I not take mine ease in mine inn?"

THE CITY OF FLOWERS—CHARACTERISTICS OF THE PEOPLE.

The captivated fancy of the visiting stranger has given to Greensboro the name of "City of Flowers," and the welcoming host who leads him, through trim parterres, a wealth of foliage and a profusion of flowers, across the hospitable threshold, fixes the colors of the charming picture with all the refinements of cultured home-life. If the love of flowers be the indication of not only an æsthetic taste but of a high moral nature, these are surely good people, for their greenhouses seem as dear to them as their dwellings, and their gardens are tended with more than the zealous care that watches over the golden harvest of the husbandman.

Many elegant residences adorn the principal streets, and if the architecture is not always fashioned strictly after approved and classic models, it is ever beautiful and attractive, with the additional merits of comfort and convenience.

Greensboro is an eminently conservative community—nor could its citizens well be otherwise, for their fathers were a homogeneous people, fostering the same traditions and cherishing the same modest aims and aspirations; here lived, and still live, the Quakers and the Nicolites, whose impress is ever strong where they move and have their being. This generation deems it best, even for a new South, to "prove all things: hold fast that which is good;" and while it would be difficult to imagine them in the vortex of a feverish "boom," losing their heads over new methods and new ideas, it would be still more difficult to imagine them given over to indifference and apathy in the face of progress and substantial improvement.

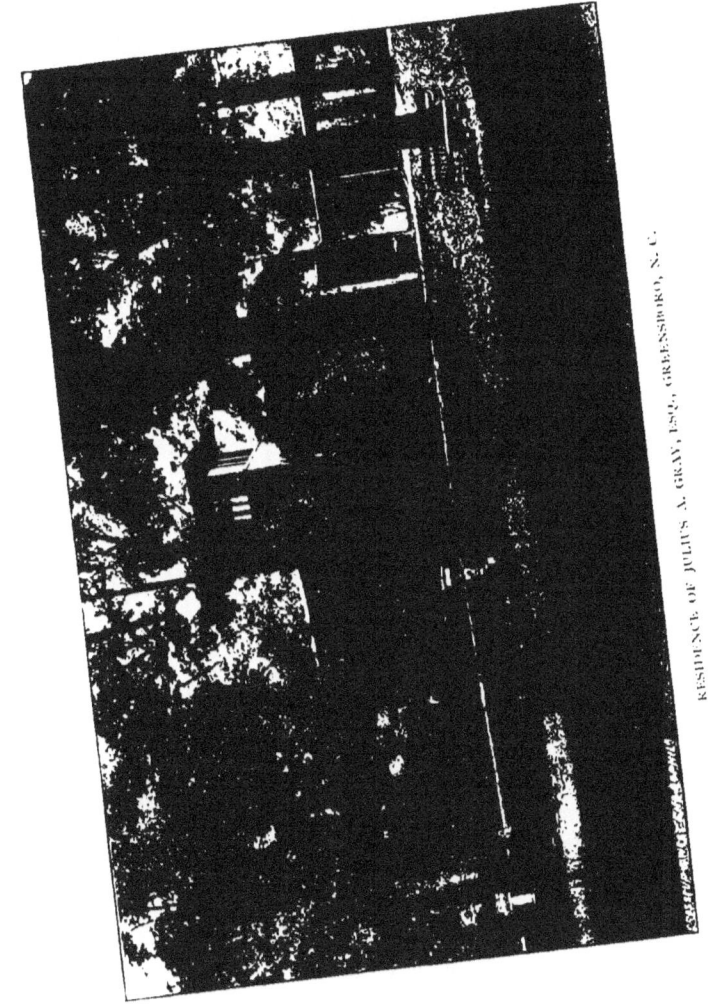

RESIDENCE OF JULIUS A. GRAY, ESQ., GREENSBORO, N. C.

MISCELLANEOUS.

Just beyond the northwestern limits of the town is Green Hill Cemetery, occupying a commanding position which overlooks the city, and here has recently been placed, with fitting ceremonies, a bronze statue of the Confederate Soldier—an admirable work of art, where, on each lineament of the strife-worn veteran, war's grim tragedy is traced.

There are published in Greensboro one daily and three weekly newspapers, and one monthly (college) magazine.

In close proximity to the depot of the road are the offices of the president of the Cape Fear and Yadkin Valley Railway, general superintendent, chief engineer, and their assistants. These occupy a commodious and handsome building, with adjoining valuable property.

The country immediately surrounding Greensboro is not only very productive of fine fruits for shipment abroad and home consumption, but is largely devoted to the growth of all kinds of fruit trees adapted to climate and soil, and there are numerous large nurseries within a radius of eight miles—in fact, this whole section is one of the great fruit nurseries of the South. Some idea of the extent of this business may be gained from the statement of the fact that the freight charges on fruit-tree shipments from this point annually aggregate from $7,000 to $8,000.

A great increase has also been recently made in the growth of greenhouse and exotic flowers, the large Pomona Nurseries in the vicinity of the city having constructed extensive greenhouses and made varied plantings of trees and shrubs for the trade in floriculture. Not only this, but the great advantages offered for grazing by the lowlands and the territory bordering the streams have given an impetus to grazing and stock-raising, and there is every probability that Guilford will soon be ranked as one of the "dairy" counties of the State.

VIEW ON ARARAT RIVER.

Piedmont and Mountain Division.

FROM GREENSBORO TO MT. AIRY—SEVENTY MILES.

TRAVERSED by this division are a portion of Guilford and the counties of Rockingham (tributary), Forsyth, Stokes and Surry. Here, indeed, is a goodly heritage of the treasures of earth and the bounties of nature waiting through the silence of centuries for development at the hands of man. All through the western and northern portions of Guilford county, fringing the sinuous banks of Haw River, stretch majestic forests, never yet profaned by the touch of the woodman's ax; clinging to the spurs and reaching up from the defiles of the Suaratown Mountains, and overshadowing with their boundless canopy the valleys of the Yadkin and Ararat Rivers, are immense quantities of the different oaks, poplar, walnut, hickory, wild cherry, ash, dogwood and locust.

The soil is the red and yellow of the gneiss and granite geological formation, and is susceptible of enormous yields of the cereals, tobacco, fruits and vegetables. In the mountain section proper of this favored division are grown apples pronounced among the finest in the world, cabbage of enormous size and remarkably fine quality, while the crops of potatoes, hay, oats, rye and buckwheat are wonderful. In a country so exuberant and prolific it is not surprising that we find fine horses, cattle, and sheep; it is the natural home of the grasses—the land of the dairy and its rich products. The greater portion of this division is also part of the "Bright Tobacco Belt;" and, although its culture has increased very rapidly within the past few years, the development of the tobacco resources of this fertile region has hardly begun.

MINERALS.

No part of North Carolina excels this section in the extent and value of its iron deposits. Through the centre of the first county in the division—Guilford—stretches a range of magnetic ore for more than twenty-five miles, than which no higher grade can be found anywhere in the world, and which is now constantly shipped to the furnaces of the North by rail. The same high grade magnetic ore is found near Danbury, in Stokes county, and immense quantities lie along the Yadkin River. Dr. Lesley, State Geologist of Pennsylvania, is high authority for the statement that "the purity of the Guilford county ore is absolute, none of it containing either sulphur or phosphorus. As to the titanium, its presence makes no difficulty under judicious furnace management. As to its quantity, centuries of heavy mining could not exhaust it."

In three analyses of the ore of Great Bend and in the vicinity of the Pilot Mountain, there was of sulphur, none; of phosphorus, 0.04, 0.05, 0.04.

MANUFACTURING.

We are treating now of a new country, awakened to a progressive life less than a year ago, and its advancement in milling, manufacturing and other pursuits is yet to come. Though inferior to that of the Cape Fear and Deep River sections, the water-power of this division is extensive and unfailing. The Ararat and its tributary creeks would more than supply the motive power for dozens of mills supporting a population of thousands.

THE MADISON BRANCH.

From Stokesdale a branch of the Cape Fear and Yadkin Valley Railway has been nearly completed to Madison, in Rockingham county, giving facilities of freight and travel to that flourishing town and to a country rich in grain resources and tobacco. The bridge across the river is rapidly constructing, and trains will be running into Madison by the 1st of June, 1889, although there has been for four months a regular schedule taking freight and passengers up to the banks of the river.

WALNUT COVE.

No place on the line has evinced a more gratifying spirit of progress than Walnut Cove, and its improvement in every branch of business and industry is very noticeable. It has the good fortune to possess citizens of energy, who know the advantages vouchsafed to them and are prompt to utilize them. Besides a considerable mercantile trade, the tobacco business employs many operatives, and puts in circulation a large amount of ready money in the payment of wages. Tanneries, flour and grist mills, &c., are also thriving industries at this point. Walnut Cove offers the right sort of welcome to the stranger in an excellent hotel, than which no town can have a better advertisement.

Connection between Winston and Walnut Cove has been recently made by the Roanoke and Southern Railroad, the contemplated extension of which leads it via Martinsville to Roanoke, Va.

FLAT ROCK, NEAR MT. AIRY, N. C.

DANBURY.

Hardly a town in the State can cherish more reasonable hopes of a bright future than Danbury, in Stokes county, distant eleven miles from the Cape Fear and Yadkin Valley Railway. The energies of those thrifty people find employment in a good general merchandise business, besides that accruing from the output of numerous large tobacco factories, tanneries, flour and corn mills, and the building which the progress of the town demands.

The tributary country is productive, but wild, broken and precipitous, and one would feel no surprise at the catastrophe which might happen to a farmer of this region, like that related by Mark Twain of the Swiss agriculturist on the Alps, who, while hoeing in his field, fell off his farm and broke his neck. But it is a "diamond in the rough," for the earth's bosom heaves tumultuously in the plenitude of its hidden wealth. Immense deposits exist here of iron, limestone, asbestos, mica, soapstone, lead, potter's clay, plumbago, beryl, &c. This profusion of mineral resources, as they are fully developed, cannot fail to make that region populous and prosperous, establishing and multiplying all kinds of manufacturing industries.

PIEDMONT SPRINGS.

Between two and three miles from Danbury are Piedmont Springs, with chalybeate waters of very fine curative qualities. This is a delightful resort, attracting crowds of visitors, both of invalids who seek the restoration of health, and of those who desire to participate in its many social pleasures and attractions. The new Piedmont Hotel was ready for the reception of guests on the 15th of May, 1889—an elegant structure of imposing exterior, and fitted up with all the conveniences pertaining to the best modern hotels.

Moore's alum and iron spring in the same vicinity has also for years been esteemed by hundreds who have tested the efficacy of its waters.

GERMANTON.

Germanton is a pretty town, beautifully located, and affording ample evidences of the thrifty and progressive spirit of its people. It draws a lucrative trade from a good farming section, and its tobacco business is especially large and daily increasing. Saw and planing mills, flour and grist mills, and several lime-kilns are busy and profitable industries. The Germanton people take pride in their town and the great advantages of their section; the social attractions and school and church facilities of the place are fine.

Near Germanton are very extensive beds of the best limestone, now worked at an excellent profit. The following analysis was furnished in 1886 by Dr. Charles W. Dabney, director of the North Carolina Experiment Station:—

    Carbonate of Lime.................................95.07
    Matter insoluble in acids.............................4.93

Summerfield, Stokesdale, Belew's Creek, Rural Hall, Dalton, Pinnacle, Pilot Mountain, Ararat, are all thriving stations—shipping points for tobacco, timber, mineral ores and country products. Rural Hall has recently been connected with Winston by the Richmond and Danville Railroad, which will doubtless accomplish much in the development of the surrounding country.

MOUNT AIRY.

Mount Airy, the present western terminus of the Cape Fear and Yadkin Valley Railway, is in Surry county, within five miles of the nearest point on the base of the Blue Ridge, with an elevation of about eleven hundred feet above sea level. Long a thriving village and the trade centre of a large and prosperous agricultural community, its growth and increase in business, industrial enterprises and population have been almost unprecedented since 1880, the census of which year gave it a population of five hundred and nineteen, increased during the past eight years to fifteen hundred.

This gratifying progress has been especially noticeable during the past four or five years, when the completion of the road to Greensboro, and its steady extension onward, gave the people of this section an undeniable guarantee of speedy railway connection with Middle and Eastern North Carolina and the great world beyond. They set their house in order for its coming, and the old political shibboleth of "the mountains ablaze" was exchanged for the better one of the fires kindled in the factories and machine-shops along the mountain-sides; the simplicity of rural life did not draw them aloof from the opportunities of material advancement, and the grandeur of their abiding-place and the copious gifts of nature enlarged their views, for—

      "Serene, not sullen, even the solitudes
        Of this unsighing people of the woods."

Mercantile business straightway received a forward impetus; building lots were in eager demand at enhanced prices; the tools of the architect and artisan were plied without ceasing; hotel accommodations were enlarged and improved; the prospect of accessibility to the great outside markets was a stimulus to the agriculture of the tributary region, and the railway celebration of June 20th, 1888, assembled thousands of visitors to behold a goodly flourishing town, with regular thoroughfares, handsome residences and blocks of commodious stores.

FLAT ROCK, NEAR MEADS, N. C.

To-day, the industries of Mt. Airy and the vicinity embrace four cotton factories, three woolen mills, eleven tobacco factories (including cigars), four tobacco sales-warehouses, three wagon factories, four grist and four saw mills, machine and blacksmith shops, &c.

The future prosperity of Mt. Airy is to be commensurate with the extent to which its people utilize the facilities for manufacturing within their reach. Almost within the corporate limits of the town, on Ararat River and Stewart's and Lovell's Creeks, are eight water-powers of from fourteen to eighteen feet head, and ample volume of water, furnishing in the aggregate from ten hundred to twelve hundred horse-power. Laurel Bluff Cotton Mills, situated a little more than a mile from town, runs two thousand spindles and forty-five looms, manufacturing plaids and warp-yarn, and employing fifty-five operatives—native labor. The brick for the building was made on the spot from the clay taken from the excavation; wood is placed at the door at one dollar per cord; satisfactory hands can be obtained at forty cents per day; and, although the cotton is bought in Charlotte and Fayetteville, this mill can afford to make its goods at prices that would be unprofitable under less favorable conditions.

As a summer resort Mt. Airy cannot fail to gain most favorable notice and win popularity with tourists as each year goes by. The salubrity of the climate, whose breezes, cooled on the rarefied heights of peak and knob and lofty ridge, come laden with the healthful balsamic odors of the mountain fir and pine; the matchless scenery of towering, blue-curtained height, deep valley, rock-girt ravine and embowered glade; the profusion of creature comforts—rich cream and butter, fresh meats, poultry, fruits and vegetables— all render this an abode of restful ease and enjoyment.

The new Blue Ridge Hotel, with a front of one hundred and twenty-five feet, containing about one hundred rooms, embellished with every attraction and furnished with every convenience, will be ready for the reception of health and pleasure seekers by the opening of the summer season of 1889.

FLAT ROCK.

Distant but a short ride from Mt. Airy is "Flat Rock," a wonder of nature in this land teeming with objects of interest. A magnificent bed of granite nearly forty acres in extent lies above the surface of the earth, ready to the hand and tool of the workman. The stone splits in great slabs, and is quarried with remarkable ease and little expense, without the aid of blasting powder. Immense quantities are daily transported over the line of railway to different points for building, masonry, paving, &c. A year or two ago a single piece of this stone was worked out from the quarry ninety-two feet in length, but this has been recently excelled by an unbroken monolith one hundred and fourteen feet long.

Every cubic foot of masonry for the magnificent iron bridge over the Cape Fear River at Fayetteville, more than one-eighth of a mile in length, is transported the distance of one hundred and sixty-seven miles from a splendid quarry near Flat Rock and more convenient to the railroad.

WHITE SULPHUR SPRINGS.

About midway between Mt. Airy and the foot of the Blue Ridge are the "White Sulphur Springs," offering comfortable hotel buildings, good rooms and wholesome fare, and they are liberally patronized by those who appreciate the medicinal efficacy of the water, an analysis of which is very similar to that of the famous Greenbrier White Sulphur Springs of Virginia.

The tobacco lands of this immediate section are unsurpassed, the grasses grow luxuriantly, fine crops of corn are raised on the alluvial soil along the streams, and the small grains give excellent harvests. No finer apple can be found in any market than that produced here, while the "Mt. Airy cabbage" (grown on the Blue Ridge slopes) is already eagerly inquired for in the Wilmington, Fayetteville and Greensboro markets.

Wheeler, in his history, credits Holman's Ford, near Wilkesboro, with the honor of being the home of Daniel Boone, the great Kentucky pioneer; but the Surry people insist that here at least was his hunting-ground and the scene of many of his exploits. Certain it is that the old inhabitants have stored in memory, through tradition and story, minute accounts of the prowess and skill of Boone, Findley, Monay, Holden and their comrades.

Within a few miles of this pleasant town married, lived and died the Siamese Twins, leaving children who are now reputable citizens of the community, but who exhibit very plainly the Mongol type in face, form and mental characteristics. This will be of interest to the curious reader, as illustrating the strange vicissitudes of fortune in this life: Taken from the semi-barbarism of the Southern Pacific Ocean, to be the wonder of gaping crowds and the study of scientific men, these strange beings ended life in right orthodox fashion—having consummated marriage under Christian ordinances, and passed years of prosaic existence as well-to-do mountain farmers in one of the commonwealths of the most enlightened republic on earth.

ASCENT OF PINNACLE OF PILOT MOUNTAIN

Scenery of the Route.

NATURE, which has been so lavish of her bounties through all the great area of territory traversed by the Cape Fear and Yadkin Valley Railway—his own prolific "vine and fig tree" to the patriarch, bursting sheaves of golden grain to the sower and reaper, the dashing water-ways of a smiling land to the spinner and weaver, and for the miner the heaped-up treasures of the earth's bosom—has interwoven with all charming pictures of mountain, glade, forest and coast.

A ride of an hour or two from its eastern terminus, by rail, steamer or carriage, places the traveler in the presence of the ocean's sublimity and "boundless immensity;" while, so far away that they seem as white-winged, fluttering birds, spreading sails ride upon the billows, and steamers plow broad furrows through the briny way. Beyond the dazzling white sand, and far away across the outjutting strips of salt marsh, lie the dismantled battlements and casemates of Forts Fisher and Caswell, where the drowsy sentinel dozed away his watch in the "piping times of peace," or cordons of bombarding ships, breached walls and thousands of tons of hissing, hurtling shells emphasized the terrible magnificence of war.

For miles beyond Wilmington the Cape Fear and Yadkin Valley Railway runs through the "low country," where grow the water, live and white oaks, of sturdy trunk and wide-spreading branches, draped in the gray river moss, whose light, graceful festoons sway softly with every passing wind. Splendid groves of this beautiful tree are common throughout this region, never without these fleecy wreaths of moss, and the effect is indescribably pleasing.

The gloom of dense morass and impenetrable swamp which fringe the copious streams that water this division is relieved by the luxuriant growth of plant and clinging vine, which in summer charm the eye with the bright colors of innumerable wild flowers and fill the air with fragrance. The sweet bay and, more rarely, the magnolia are found throughout all these lowland forests.

MOORE'S CREEK BATTLE-GROUND.

On the line of the road, in New Hanover County, near the mouth of Moore's Creek, is the battle-ground of that name, where, on the 27th of February, 1776, the Royalists were so severely defeated by an inferior force under Colonels Caswell and Lillington. In this engagement Captain McDonald, the husband of

Flora, was taken prisoner—the first stroke of hapless fortune which followed them to the end, and prompted Flora McDonald to exclaim that she "had served, at the risk of life, both the House of Stuart and the House of Hanover, and was not much the gainer by either."

The country embraced in the upper Cape Fear and Deep River sections is without notable and striking beauties of scenery, beyond the great stretches of noble forests, the winding streams, and the broad acres of a thrifty agricultural people. Utterly lacking in the picturesque, the long-leaf pine, to the stranger beholding it for the first time, is invested with a peculiar interest. A great orchard or plantation (as it is called) of pine worked for turpentine possesses singular features belonging to it alone. The great height of the trees, with their resinous trunks and boxes; their remarkable regularity, which permits long vistas of perspective through the forest; the strange bunches of needles (the pine's sole foliage), which repeat the "song of the wind" in a soft, murmuring sough, have upon the eye and the imagination a pleasant and soothing effect.

GUILFORD BATTLE-GROUND.

Five miles west of Greensboro is the battle-ground of Guilford Court-house, where, on the 15th of March, 1781, Gen. Nathaniel Greene and his army met the forces of Cornwallis in a hard-fought engagement, which destroyed the foothold of British power in this State, and was the beginning of the end of the prestige and supremacy of British arms in America. To a distinguished and patriotic citizen of the city of Greensboro the people of North Carolina are indebted for invaluable service in rescuing the fame of our troops on that field from unmerited reproach—service which has been recognized by an annual appropriation to the battle-ground by the General Assembly of the State, to be followed probably by a still larger appropriation for a monument by the United States Government. The battle-ground is kept in admirable order, and is beautified with monuments, shaded walks, gushing springs, neat cottages, a museum of revolutionary relics, &c. The stirring events which render the spot historic are annually celebrated in May by a grand pageant and oration.

PILOT MOUNTAIN.

Nearly midway on the line of the Piedmont and Mountain Division is the Pilot Mountain, with an altitude of twenty-four hundred and fifty-eight feet, whose summit is capped by the Pinnacle, an irregular cylindrical or truncated cone-shaped mass of rock with a surface area of about half an acre. The Pilot is divided into two parts—cleft asunder, doubtless, by some convulsion of nature in past ages, the lesser mountain merging gradually into the hills beyond. The

VIEW ON MADAM RIVER

ascent to the Pinnacle is easy, and the latter is mounted by stone steps and ladders; during the dizzy climb the guide does not fail to tell you that fair woman comes to the accomplishment of this feat of the tourist with a leveler head than protecting man; she rarely fails to mount to the top, while her escort, as often as not, surveys the towering height—and takes his seat at the base to await the return of the party. Accompanying illustrations give beautiful views of the mountain from different points on the road. *Piloting* the Indian, in centuries past, through the trackless wilds of his hunting-grounds, standing alone in nature's vast expanse, it still keeps watch and ward over hamlet, village and field—the fruits of a civilization which has brought the steel rail and the rushing train, paying its passing tribute in the long trail of the engine's smoke that floats upward and curtains its rugged sides.

The Suaratown Mountains lie off to the right of the Cape Fear and Yadkin Valley Railway—a range of lofty hills presenting varied and charming pictures of the graceful, beautiful and picturesque.

ARARAT RIVER.

Here the scenery assumes a character of wild and rugged grandeur which finds its counterpart only in the majestic pictures of the transmontane region. The road winds through deep cuts and precipitous defiles, hugging the sides of the hills—

"Rock-ribbed and ancient as the sun,"

and flanked by the Ararat River's tortuous channel and rocky bed. Engineering skill has here triumphed over wonderful obstacles, and the traveler is struck by the many points of similarity presented by this portion of the route and parts of the Pennsylvania Central Railroad beyond the "Horseshoe."

THE BLUE RIDGE.

The present western terminus of the road offers a grand view of the main chain of the Blue Ridge Mountains, which to the north have a height of nearly three-fourths of a mile; two miles distant is the beautiful Slate Mountain, and, farther on, Little Mountain, a great spur from the main range; to the southeast the beauties of the Suaratown Mountains charm the eye as the mists of morning clear away, and the Pilot looms grandly in the distance.

The extension of the Cape Fear and Yadkin Valley Railway, and its connection with the Norfolk and Western beyond the State line, will furnish to the voyager the scenery of a wild mountain country in its perfection, and the surmounting and passage of the Blue Ridge will carry him through the wonders attending the construction of railway under such circumstances as will find their parallel in those about Round Knob.

OLD-STYLE COTTON PRESS, NEAR GULF, N. C.

Recapitulation.

HE compiler of this work has followed the line of the Cape Fear and Yadkin Valley Railway from tidewater to the foot of the Blue Ridge, noting carefully and gathering steadily in his examination of the resources of the country developed by the line. Except where he has felt justified in using approximate figures in his estimate of the increase of population since the last census, he has aimed to deal only in plain *facts*, and if there is aught inaccurate or untrue within these pages, he does not know of it. That the road is well worthy of the important place assigned to it by the people of North Carolina among the great internal improvements of the South, is shown by the following summary of statistical information:—

It leads from northwest to southeast, through a belt of nineteen counties, sustaining a population of 363,572, embraced in a territory of 12,759 square miles, or 8,165,760 square acres, improved and unimproved, with a total tax valuation of $22,933,045, and a real and personal property valuation of $48,572,417. The rate of taxation in this State is remarkably low; were it anything like that of the Eastern and Middle States, the above figures would be increased from $22,933,045 to at least $45,000,000, and from $48,572,417 to $60,000,000.

This broad domain grows an infinite variety of agricultural products: corn, wheat, rye, oats (of which the midland and western sections raise a surplus), rice, peanuts, Irish and sweet potatoes, field-peas, chufas, sorghum, cotton, tobacco, and every garden vegetable produced from one end of the Atlantic coast to the other. Of fruits, the whole region is especially prolific: the pomegranate, white and blue fig, a greater number of distinct species of grapes than can be found in any other Southern State, apricots, nectarines, the Japan plum, apples, pears, peaches, plums, cherries, delicious melons, and all the small fruits in profusion. So diversified are the products throughout the extent of the line, and so marked are the climatic differences, that an agreeable and profitable interchange of commodities is possible between the people of one region and the other—those of the tidewater and low country tendering to their friends of the Piedmont and mountain section the first fruits of their labors in early spring, vegetables of all kinds, while yet stern nature holds locked in her embrace forest and field and glade of the up-country. Thence shall come, when the earlier seasons of the coast have brought their treasures and passed away, the offerings quickened into luxuriant growth by mountain breeze and clime: apples, pears, peaches, cherries, the Blue Ridge cabbage (the finest in the world), and the dairy products of this goodly land.

The strides made in manufacturing have been rapid; but, in comparison with the magnificent possibilities furnished by the water-power along the line, the establishment of the different branches of skilled industry may be said to have hardly commenced. Besides cotton milling, the almost inexhaustible forest area renders easy and feasible the manufacture of nearly everything useful in wood: wheels, hubs, spokes, handles, shuttles, buckets, furniture, the wooden gear of agricultural implements, and, in fine, all the woodenwares entering into the daily domestic and business employments of man. Iron and coal—the quality and quantity of which have been attested by unimpeachable authority—offer abundant material and unusual facilities for the establishment of foundries and the manufacture of car and carriage wheels and axles, plows, axes, the different tools of the artisan, &c.

Collateral advantages combine to make this one of the favored manufacturing districts of the world: the raw material is easy of access by the mills; fuel can be obtained at a merely nominal price at the doors of the factories; the general mildness of the climate admits of uninterrupted labor all the year round; there is no restless element, infected by "strikes" and fomenting discontent; an intelligent population are quick to learn the trades, and are soon adepts at the loom, the spindle and the engine-wheel.

The writer was careful to question the proprietors of the different mills herein described as to whether native labor was employed, and whether it was satisfactory, and in nearly every instance an affirmative reply has been given.

MINERALS.

Red and brown sandstone, a superior quality of granite, soapstone, gold, coal and iron exist in quarries, beds, mines, deposits and ranges in the two upper divisions of the Cape Fear and Yadkin Valley Railway—the last two not only of paramount importance in their application to the useful arts of man, but constantly demanded in all his industrial avocations and the round of his daily life. What may we not expect in the future from the full utilization of the unparalleled riches of this section!

TIMBER RESOURCES.

Nearly all the different kinds of timber found in the shipyards of the great markets of this country grow immediately upon or contiguous to the line of this railway: the pine (alone worth millions of dollars annually in

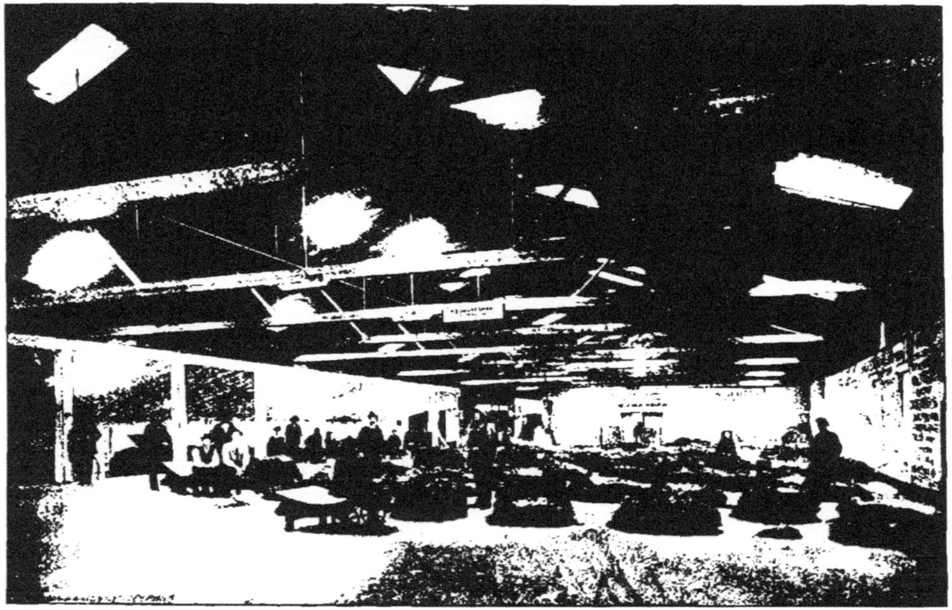

TOBACCO WAREHOUSE, GREENSBORO, N.C.

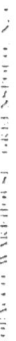

lumber and naval stores), all the species of oak, cedar, holly, cherry, cypress, juniper, hickory, dogwood, walnut, sycamore, persimmon, elm, gum, chestnut, beech, locust, ash, maple and other less important woods.

The lesser plant *flora* is also rich and varied, the lower counties producing many shrubs and flowers, which make it one of the most remunerative honey-producing sections of North Carolina, while in the mountainous counties are found many valuable medicinal herbs, which are gathered in very considerable quantity, and constitute a profitable industry.

A GREAT COMMERCIAL HIGHWAY.

No better summing-up could be made of the "natural indications of this route as the necessary track of a commercial highway" than by the following terse quotation from an esteemed authority:—

"It is the shortest line to the head of navigation (and outlet by sea) for almost the whole middle and Piedmont regions of the State. This has been, and always must be, a most weighty consideration in settling the permanent channels of traffic. It lies, its whole length, through a region whose climate never affects traffic for a day in the year. It crosses at right angles three great north and south railroad lines, and so makes them also feeders to its freight supplies."

INDUCEMENTS FOR INVESTMENT.

In all the nineteen counties included in this route good farming lands can be procured at from five dollars to twenty dollars per acre. Excellent water-powers are to be obtained at reasonable figures, while in the cities, towns and villages real estate is held at moderate prices. Almost universally good water, a salubrious climate, a satisfactory system of hired labor, law-abiding and intelligent communities, enjoying as good church and school advantages as limited means and a sparse population will permit—all combine to make this an attractive land and a pleasant home to the industrious settler from any quarter of the globe.

The Transmontane Extension.

AVING accomplished this great work within the borders of the State; almost tracking the sands of the coast at its eastern terminus; traversing the bottoms and gently undulating uplands of the Cape Fear section; pushing aside the obstacles of boulder and rock through the rugged midland region, and climbing undauntedly onward up to the crowning, lofty gateway leading into the great valley of the West; having at length brought to its fruition the Cape Fear and Yadkin Valley system:--shall the barriers of mountain and gorge stay its further progress? Shall not, rather, the aggressive Western civilization hail its coming, and greet its forward movement with connections to the great highway of travel and traffic on to Cincinnati?

But a few miles remain between the present western terminus of the road and the State line, beyond which it is placed in direct communication with a broad valley, or, rather, a succession of valleys of wonderful fertility, immense resources and vast natural wealth. Meeting it from the rich pasture and stock-raising lands of Southwest Virginia, the Norfolk and Western Railroad would carry it on to the treasures of a country fairer, if possible, in East Tennessee, whence further connections would open to its transportation the almost untouched riches of Southeastern Kentucky. To him who has but cursorily glanced at the products of this "full-blooded heart of the continent," the bare statement of facts must seem the language of extravagance. Occupying an area equal in extent to one-fifth of the territory of North Carolina, the coal fields of Eastern Kentucky, with all the fertile and diversified region, including Southwest Virginia, are reasonably sure to become the centre of a great iron industry. Extensive deposits of coal, in beds ranging from fifteen to twenty feet in thickness, in conjunction with immense ranges of iron ore, cannot fail to make this a country abounding in varied and profitable industries.

But this is only a tithe of the wealth awaiting utilization and development in this fair valley. While from its skirts ascends the smoke of hundreds of smelting furnaces, it holds in its lap a granary for almost a world's consumption. The agricultural products seem to be without limit. Corn and all the small grains, the products of the dairy and the orchard, besides salt, plaster and great droves of fine horses, mules and cattle—now conveyed by toilsome means and roundabout ways to the extreme Southern States and the Northern markets — would then furnish all the year through an amount of freight which would tax the most extensive railway transportation facilities, for this route would offer the most speedy and direct transit to the Atlantic slope and the seacoast.

The unfinished part of the line of the Cape Fear and Yadkin Valley Railway is by an excellent route of about five miles to the State border, and connection will probably be made with the Norfolk and Western Railroad at Willis' Gap. When once this direct communication is made, it must inevitably be followed by connections which will graft it permanently upon the great chain of railway lines extending through the Cumberland Valley to Louisville and Knoxville, and onward to the great Western States by the South Atlantic and Ohio and Charleston, Cumberland Gap and Chicago Railroads.

When we take into consideration the mineral wealth abounding throughout the great plateau of Western North Carolina, either on the line of the Cape Fear and Yadkin Valley Railway or within easy connection thereto :—the vast magnetite iron ranges, including the rich and extensive Cranberry deposits, and extending eastward to the great beds of Stokes, Guilford and Chatham—the great industries to be speedily developed by the transmontane extension will find their parallel only in the most flourishing manufacturing districts of the country. The demand for coke in the manufacture of iron and steel—often hitherto transported from one thousand to twelve hundred miles to the smelting furnaces—is increasing year by year in tremendous ratio, and the western extension lays the shortest and quickest line of rail between coal bed and iron deposit, bringing together by easy transportation all the materials for the successive steps of iron and steel manufacture.

In the preparation and arrangement of these pages the difficulty has been not to gather material, but to summarize and compress that material into convenient form ; an "embarrassment of riches" rather than a poverty of resources meets the compiler of the great and diversified resources developed by the Cape Fear and Yadkin Valley Railway. Do not the abundant facts presented justify the claim that no road in the South offers superior advantages or holds out brighter promise of progress and prosperity to the region through which it passes ? Judicious investment of capital in manufacturing enterprises for the utilization of the varied resources of this favored land will make bustling cities of the towns, and thriving towns of the villages and hamlets which dot the line of road from border to border of the State ; immigration will bring an industrious population to augment the wealth and producing power of thrifty communities ; and the near future will bring the realization of the long-cherished dream of the completion of the

North Carolina Cape Fear and Yadkin Valley System.

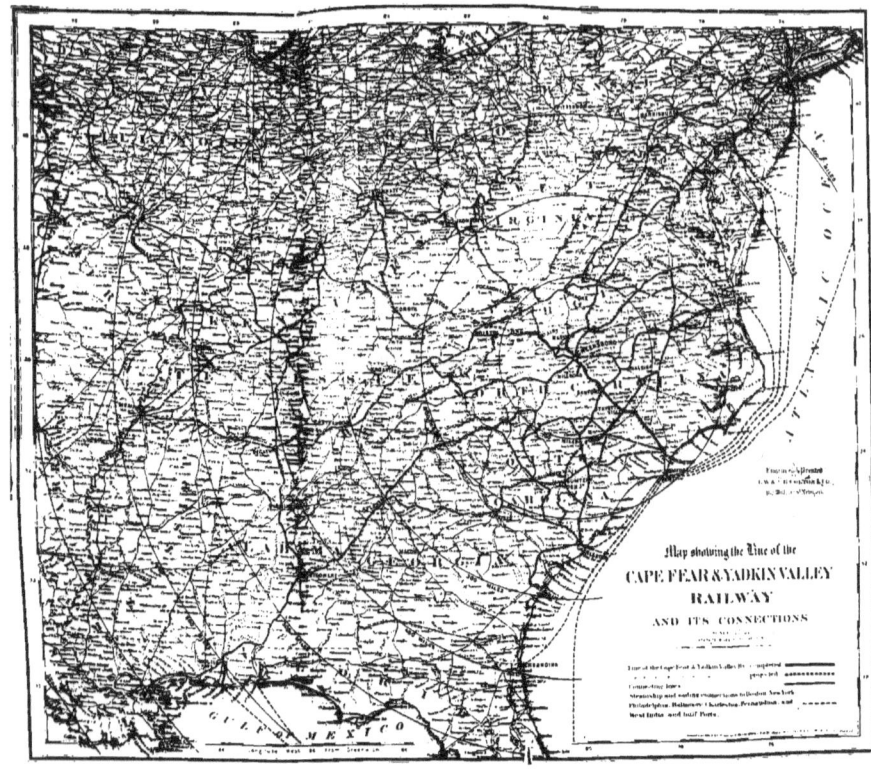

www.ingramcontent.com/pod-product-compliance
Lightning Source LLC
Chambersburg PA
CBHW020135170426
43199CB00010B/746